the
baby&toddler
cookbook

Authors   Karen Ansel, MS, RD & Charity Ferreira

Photographer   Thayer Allyson Gowdy

weldon**owen**

Contents

About this book

Of the many milestones of baby's first year, starting solids is an adventure you'll never forget. Some days, you'll be met with an eager mouth that's wide open, and giggles and squeals of delight. On others, you may encounter lips tightly pursed shut, cereal bowls turned upside down, and sippy cups knocked to the floor.

Yet with love, patience, and a steady supply of nutritious food, you can have a profound impact on this journey. In fact, nobody has a greater influence on your child's eating habits than you do. By offering baby a wide variety of healthful, tasty foods, you can help her become a well-rounded and adventurous eater.

Why homemade?

Choosing to prepare homemade food for your baby lets you decide exactly what goes into it. That's not to say you'll never reach for a jar of baby food on busy days or in a pinch, but making baby's meals fresh from your kitchen is one of the best gifts you can give her.

Better nutrition

When you prepare baby's food yourself, you know it's free of unnecessary additives like starches, thickeners, and preservatives. You can also control things that baby doesn't need, like sugar and salt. Home-cooked baby food allows you to use seasonal ingredients packed with flavor and harvested at their nutritional peak. While it might take a little extra effort, making homemade food is easier than you might think, especially because you

can make it in large batches from ingredients that are already in your kitchen, and then store it for later meals. That allows you to feed baby many of the same foods that the rest of the family is eating and can also save you money.

Better taste

Baby food that you make in your kitchen tastes better because it's fresher. Cooking from scratch also allows you to offer baby a wider variety of ingredients, since not all foods are available as commercial baby food. That means she'll learn to eat many different kinds of fruits, vegetables, grains, and proteins, as well as aromatics, herbs, spices, and your selection of the best-quality, free-range, antibiotic-free meats. By exposing her to many different kinds of flavors early on, she'll be more likely to try and accept new and different foods later as a toddler.

Better texture

You can also make sure the texture is just right. This is especially important because the textures of foods are as new to baby as the flavors. At first, you can thin baby's food with breast milk or formula. Then, as she becomes a more adept eater, you can make it thicker and chunkier so it's just right for each stage she passes through.

Starting solids

Until now, breast milk or iron-fortified formula has given baby all the nutrition he needs to grow and thrive. But as he nears six months of age, his digestive system begins to mature, and he is now able to digest solid foods.

When is baby ready?

At six months, baby is physically starting to develop the skills he needs to transition to solid foods. But how do you know when he is ready to take his first spoonful? The best way is to follow his lead and watch for the following signs:

- Baby can sit upright with support.
- He holds his head steady.
- He will open his mouth or lean forward when food is offered in front of him.
- He can swallow food when it is placed in his mouth instead of pushing it back out.
- He is interested in what you are eating.

Complementary foods

Even though baby may be ready for solid foods, breast milk or iron-fortified formula will still be the mainstay of his diet. In fact, a baby who is just starting solids may eat only a few teaspoons at each sitting.

Complementary foods such as pureed squash, rice cereal, and applesauce do more than just provide added nutrition—they help baby learn how to eat, chew, and swallow food and to accept and adapt to new tastes and textures.

Breast is still best

Breast milk is nature's perfect first food and the best nutritional start. In fact, health experts recommend breast-feeding your baby exclusively for his first six months, if possible, and then offering both breast milk and solids until at least age one.

The benefits of breast-feeding include the following:

- Breast milk provides antibodies that help protect baby against illness and infection.
- Breast-fed babies have fewer tummy troubles. Mother's milk is easier for them to digest than formula and encourages the development of baby's digestive system.
- The flavors from the foods you eat are passed into your milk, exposing baby to a wide range of flavors.
- Breast milk contains beneficial fats that enhance mental development.
- Breast-feeding also protects against the development of food allergies, obesity, diarrhea, and ear and respiratory infections.

New foods at every stage

Over the next few months, you will slowly help your baby progress from thinned purees to table food. Here's what you can expect:

4 to 6 months

- Single-grain cereals such as rice, barley, millet, or oats that have been thinned with breast milk or formula; supplementing these cereals, which are high in minerals, fiber, protein, and B vitamins, with iron-rich formula or breast milk will help ensure that your baby gets the iron he needs to support his rapid growth

- Pureed sweet, low-acid fruits like apples and pears, and starchy-sweet vegetables such as peas and sweet potatoes

7 to 8 months

- A wider range of fruit and vegetable purees, including brightly flavored fruits like peaches, plums, and cherries, and earthy-tasting vegetables like beets, asparagus, mushrooms, and green beans

- Combinations of purees using any of the ingredients baby has been introduced to so far, to broaden baby's taste for flavors

- Coarser—and sometimes chunky, if baby can handle it—purees of cereals, vegetables, fruits, and meats to familiarize baby with different textures and to initiate chewing

- High-protein, soft-cooking legumes such as lentils and split peas

- A touch of added fats (butter, olive oil) to add flavor and increase the pleasant feeling of food in baby's mouth

- Baby's first meats: purees of lamb, beneficial because it's high in iron, and turkey, a good source of lean protein that's easy to digest

9 to 11 months

- Coarse, chunky, or mashed fruit, vegetable, and legume purees

- Small chunks of soft, cooked vegetables and very ripe fruits

- Whole-milk yogurt, ricotta, or cottage cheese

- Shredded semihard cheeses such as Cheddar and Monterey jack

- Finely minced meats, including chicken and pork, and egg yolks

- More herbs, spices, and aromatics such as onion and garlic

- Fruit juice—100-percent juice; should be limited to 1/4 cup (2 fl oz/60 ml) a day

1 year and up

- Table foods that the whole family is eating, such as soups and stews, pasta and noodles, or quesadillas, cut into bite-sized pieces

- Honey

- Whole cow's milk

- Fish

- Citrus fruits

- Small amounts of salt and pepper

Healthy foods for baby & toddler

From the time she starts solids until she's a toddler, your little one needs a wide variety of foods to get the nutrients she needs to grow up healthy and strong. The following table will help guide you to the best foods you can offer on her plate.

Types of food	Examples	Why baby needs them
VITAMIN C–RICH FRUITS AND VEGETABLES	Strawberries, papayas, mangoes, tomatoes, bell peppers (capsicums), and broccoli	They keep baby's immune system strong. Vitamin C also increases the absorption of iron from plant foods such as cereals and grains.
YELLOW-ORANGE FRUITS AND VEGETABLES	Cantaloupe, apricots, papayas, sweet potatoes, carrots, and winter squashes	They are rich in vitamin A for healthy eyes and skin. Vitamin A also helps fight infection.
GREEN VEGETABLES	Spinach, avocado, broccoli, and asparagus	They supply folate, which helps promote heart health, build new cells, and support growth.
WHOLE GRAINS	Oats, millet, barley, couscous, polenta, and brown rice; iron-fortified cereals; bread; crackers; pasta	Whole grains are packed with complex carbohydrates needed for energy. Iron-fortified cereals can help baby get the iron she needs, which is critical for supporting rapid growth and cognitive development during the infant and toddler years.

Types of food	Examples	Why baby needs them
BEANS AND LEGUMES	Black, cannellini, kidney, and pinto beans; chickpeas (garbanzo beans); edamame; green peas; lentils	Beans and legumes are packed with both protein and complex carbohydrates. They are also a top source of folate.
POULTRY, PORK, AND EGGS	Chicken, turkey, lean pork, and eggs	These supply protein needed for growth and to build cells, muscles, and organs. Infants and toddlers require more protein per pound of body weight now than at any other stage of their lives.
RED MEAT AND DARK-MEAT POULTRY	Dark-meat chicken and turkey, lamb, and lean cuts of beef	In addition to supplying protein and iron, these are rich in zinc needed to support growth and for a healthy immune system.
LOW-MERCURY VARIETIES OF FISH	Wild salmon, flounder, sole, freshwater trout, and white fish	Fish are excellent sources of lean protein as well as the omega-3 fatty acids DHA and EPA, which can enhance baby's cognitive development and visual acuity.
FULL-FAT DAIRY PRODUCTS	Cheese, ricotta cheese, cottage cheese, yogurt, and whole milk	These are toddler's primary source of calcium, needed to build strong bones. They are also packed with protein.

In the kitchen

With just a little advance planning and the right tools, cooking for baby can be quick and easy. Setting aside approximately 1 hour just 2 days a week can ensure that your little one will enjoy fresh, homemade food all week long.

Simple tools for cooking

Cooking for baby doesn't require specialized gadgets or appliances. In fact, it's likely that you already have all the tools that you will need in your kitchen right now. The basic equipment for cooking baby's food includes:

- A medium-sized saucepan.
- A steamer basket or insert.
- A baking pan or dish.
- A food processor or blender for pureeing. You can also puree baby's food by passing it through a food mill or pushing it through a strainer with a wooden spoon.
- A potato masher or fork, when baby is ready for chunkier foods.

Best cooking methods

Cooking methods like steaming, poaching, and roasting are best for baby's first meals. Not only are they fast and easy, but they don't require added fat, which can be difficult for his delicate system to digest.

Steamed and roasted foods have the added benefit of not coming into contact with water, which can wash away nutrients.

Organic ingredients

On a relative basis, your baby is eating more food per pound of body weight than you are, so you want to make sure it's as pure as possible. By selecting organic ingredients, you ensure that baby's diet is free of synthetic hormones, pesticides, and antibiotics, which can be harmful for an infant's developing body and brain.

The best organic fruits and vegetables to purchase are those that tend to be highest in pesticide residue.

VEGETABLES

- Bell peppers (capsicums)
- Celery
- Root vegetables, such as potatoes or carrots
- Greens, such as spinach or lettuce

FRUITS

- Peaches and nectarines
- Apples
- Strawberries
- Cherries

Keeping it safe

A well-rounded diet can give your little one all the nutrients she needs for a healthy start. But until she reaches her first birthday, there are some foods you may want to introduce carefully to minimize her risk of food allergies and foodborne illness.

Allergy awareness

Right now, baby's digestive system is still maturing. As a result, it may allow undigested proteins to pass through her digestive tract. When this happens, her body may treat these normally harmless proteins as allergens. After her first birthday, food allergies become less of a concern as her system will be mature enough to screen out most proteins. Children from families with a history of allergies may have sensitive systems, which take longer to mature. If that's the case in your family, speak with your doctor to find out if you need to delay introducing certain foods past baby's first year.

Until the one-year mark, introducing single-ingredient foods can make it easier for you to recognize if a new food is causing a reaction. After each new food, wait 3–5 days before introducing the next new food. During this time,

if you suspect a food allergy, stop feeding the offending food and speak with your pediatrician.

Although any food can cause a food allergy, the following are the most common offenders:

- Milk
- Eggs
- Wheat
- Soy
- Fish
- Shellfish
- Tree nuts
- Peanuts

Cleanliness is key

A clean kitchen ensures that baby's food will be free of germs and bacteria. Here are some tips for keeping your kitchen clean:

- Before you start preparing baby's food, wash your hands well with soap and water.

- Make sure you wash all produce thoroughly (even if it's organic or if you plan to peel it).

- Use separate work surfaces and utensils for raw meat, poultry, or seafood.

- When you are finished, promptly refrigerate or freeze baby's food and clean all workspaces and utensils with hot, soapy water.

- Once baby is finished eating, you may want to save her leftovers, but because her spoon has

Signs of an allergic reaction

- Diarrhea
- Rash
- Gassiness
- Hives
- Wheezing
- Difficulty breathing
- Vomiting

introduced germs into her bowl, it's better to throw away any food she hasn't eaten.

Preventing choking

Enthusiastic babies and young children often stuff their mouths with favorite foods, or bite off more than they can chew in one mouthful. This can cause choking accidents. You can help minimize the risk by following these guidelines:

- Sit with baby while she eats. This teaches her that meals are special family time, and if she does start to choke on her food, you'll notice right away.

- When your child is ready for finger foods, cut it into pieces no larger than ¼ inch (6 mm).

- Put only a few pieces of food on her plate or in her bowl at a time.

- Teach her to take small bites and chew her food completely.

Gassy foods

Sometimes it's difficult to tell if baby is suffering from a food allergy or simply has a case of gas. These foods may be making the problem worse:

- Dairy
- Beans
- Broccoli
- Onions
- Fruit juice
- Wheat
- Cauliflower
- Garlic

Foods to hold off on

Throughout the first year, you'll slowly introduce more and more new foods to your baby. But there are a few you may want to avoid until she's at least age one, or in some cases, age two:

RAW-MILK CHEESES Made from unpasteurized milk, these may contain harmful bacteria.

LOW-FAT DAIRY PRODUCTS Baby needs the fat from dairy products for her developing brain, so feed her full-fat dairy until age two.

SUGAR Sugar contains empty calories that fill baby up, leaving less room for nutritious foods.

SALT Before the age of one, babies don't need extra salt. Seasoning her food with salt now will only encourage a preference for salty foods later. You can add flavor to foods with small amounts of herbs and spices instead. After age one, you can start seasoning her food lightly with salt.

COW'S MILK Waiting until after baby's first birthday can lessen the chances of an allergy to milk.

UNDERCOOKED MEAT Rare or partially cooked meat, fish, poultry, and eggs

HONEY AND CORN SYRUP These may contain small amounts of botulism spores that can sicken babies younger than age one.

Introducing new foods

Offering new foods makes mealtime more nutritious for baby and more exciting for both of you. Though you may be excited to expose him to all kinds of yummy new foods, rest assured that soon enough he'll be eating along with the rest of the family. For now, while he's learning the basics, a slow, steady approach will help him adjust.

Tips for trying

Getting baby to try new foods can sometimes be a struggle. The following tips will help make things a little easier on everyone:

- Only offer one new food at a time. This will make it easier to pinpoint the culprit if your baby has a reaction.

- Since baby's taste buds can be more sensitive than adults, it's best to avoid heavy or overly spicy seasonings.

- Food can be room temperature or slightly warm, but make sure that it's not too hot.

- When giving baby a new food, offer a small amount, and realize this will be a completely new taste and texture experience for him. Even if he takes only one bite, that's fine.

- Feeding new foods along with familiar foods makes it easier for baby to accept a new food for the first time. Then, wait to see if he likes it. If he's not enthusiastic, don't force him. He may be more willing next time.

- Over time, baby's tastes will change. Don't be surprised if foods he originally had no interest in someday become his favorites.

Perfect timing

The ideal time to feed your baby is when he is well rested and happy. A good time is often in the morning, since baby can be fussy later in the day. It also helps if he is a little hungry, although you don't want him to be so hungry that he can't focus on the task at hand.

Know when to call it quits

Babies' and toddlers' appetites vary from day to day and even from meal to meal. So, it's completely normal for them to eat little at one sitting and more at another. When they are allowed to rely on their own internal fullness cues, they are usually quite adept at deciding how much or how little food they need.

Your baby should be the one to tell you when he's had enough. Recognizing the following signs of fullness can prevent power struggles and battles at the table:

- Turning his head away
- Leaning backwards
- Refusing to open his mouth
- Playing with his food

First bites

Offering baby homemade, wholesome foods ensures that her first experience with table foods will be packed with both nutrition and flavor. This chapter offers a host of recipes and cereals you can make at home from whole, single grains (such as rice, barley, oat, and millet) as well as simple, single-ingredient pureed fruits and vegetables.

Providing a variety of different tastes, colors, and textures is the ideal way to start baby on her journey to healthy eating. At first, she'll begin slowly with single-ingredient foods to help her make the transition to table food. Within just a few weeks, she'll be ready for combinations of flavors that will make her meals even more delicious and interesting.

Baby's first meals

Around the age of 6 months, your baby will probably be ready to start trying solid foods. At first, baby's meals will be more about learning how to eat than actually eating much food. In fact, at this stage she's still getting most of her nutrition from breast milk or formula and is nursing or getting a bottle at least 3–5 times a day.

Easy does it

Meal times with your baby aren't just about good nutrition. They are special times that allow you to communicate, bond, and watch her experience the joys of discovering new flavors and textures. Learning to read baby's signals will make feeding a happy time for both of you.

Eating is a completely new and different experience for baby. While you might be eager to get started, it's best to start off slowly with only one solid-food meal a day for the first month. For baby's first few meals you'll want to offer her small servings of 1 or 2 teaspoonfuls of a

single ingredient at each mealtime. Over the next few days and weeks, as she becomes accustomed to eating, she'll become increasingly ready for you to spoon up more.

Choosing the best foods

Once upon a time, parents were told to start baby on a strict diet of cereal; nowadays, it is widely thought that the order in which you introduce solids is entirely up to you. There are, of course, certain ingredients that are thought to be best for starting baby out: sweet fruits like apples and pears, mild vegetables such as butternut squash and peas, and whole-grain cereals such as rice and millet. The recipes for each of these single-ingredient purees and cereals allow you to add flavor and nutrition to baby's diet.

Keep in mind, however, that purchased iron-fortified cereal is also an important staple in baby's pantry (see "The Importance of Iron," page 40), as iron deficiency is the most common nutrient deficiency among babies and toddlers. You can ensure that you are choosing a cereal with enough iron by scanning the nutrition facts on the side of the box. Most fortified cereals will provide 45 percent of the daily value for iron.

When is baby hungry?

The best time to feed baby is when she's well rested and not fussy. Learning to read her cues can help you gauge when she's ready to eat, but before she gets too hungry (and can't focus on the task at hand). While crying is sometimes a sign of hunger in babies, baby may also open her mouth wide when she sees food, kick her legs and swing her arms, and bob her head forward.

One ingredient at a time

When starting baby out on solid foods, make sure to introduce each ingredient one at a time so you'll know if a new food disagrees with her. Since reactions to food aren't always immediate, it's best to wait 3–5 days before offering any additional new foods.

As your baby gets older and acquires a wider range of tastes, start combining the cereals and fruit and vegetable purees that you'll find in this chapter. Blending foods together adds more exciting flavors and textures to her plate. It also provides a nutritional boost by enhancing the absorption of nutrients in her food.

If you're worried that fruits will encourage a sweet tooth, don't be. Babies are born with a preference for sweet flavors. In fact, if your baby is nursing, she's been enjoying the sweet flavor of breast milk for months.

Easy to swallow

You can make first foods easier for baby to swallow by thinning her food to a liquidy consistency. Try mixing her cereal or puree with a little breast milk or formula, as these offer a familiar flavor that's likely to help win her over. Breast milk and formula also add more nutrition to the foods you are serving to baby. Over time, as she learns to swallow solids, you can slowly adjust the thickness of her food by adding less and less liquid to it.

Tips for feeding baby

Here are some simple tips for feeding your new eater, which will help make baby more comfortable and happy when mealtime comes around:

- Seat baby in a high chair or an infant seat propped with pillows so she's sitting up straight.
- Sit facing her and hold a small, long-handled spoon of food about a foot in front of her.
- Wait for baby to open her mouth. If she doesn't open her mouth, gently touch the spoon to her lips or gums.
- Let baby determine how quickly or slowly she prefers to eat and when it's time to stop eating.
- Stop feeding her when she shows signs that she's full or tired by the new activity (see page 16).

Sleeping and solids

While it is common to think that adding solid food to baby's diet will help her sleep through the night, child experts agree that it actually makes little difference. By around the age of 4 months, most babies are physically able to sleep for 6–7 hours at a time without waking up for a feeding. If your baby is still wanting to feed during the night, the cause is most likely that she's waking up out of habit, not from hunger.

Applesauce

Applesauce is not only quick and easy to make, it's extremely versatile—a natural combined with rice cereal for baby's breakfast, or savory mashes later in the day. Add a pinch of cinnamon, if your baby likes it. Avoid tart varieties like the green Pippin and Granny Smith, otherwise baby may not like it without sweetening.

6 sweet apples such as Gala, Pink Lady, or McIntosh, about 3 lb (1.5 kg) total weight, quartered and cored

MAKES ABOUT 2½ CUPS (20 FL OZ/625 ML) APPLESAUCE

- Pour water into a large saucepan to a depth of 1 inch (2.5 cm). Put the apples in a steamer basket and put the basket in the saucepan. Bring to a boil over high heat. Cover and steam until the apples are very tender, 10–12 minutes.

- Remove from the heat and remove the steamer basket from the saucepan, reserving the cooking liquid. Let the apples cool, then remove and discard the skins. Transfer the apples to a blender or food processor and process to a smooth puree. Add enough of the reserved cooking liquid, breast milk, or formula to thin the puree to a consistency your baby can handle.

STORE IT Refrigerate in an airtight container for up to 3 days, or spoon individual portions into ice-cube trays or other baby-food freezer containers and freeze, covered, for up to 3 months. (Some discoloration may occur during storage.)

FOODS TO GROW ON "An apple a day . . ." Sweet and full of fiber and vitamin C, apples are a great first fruit for baby; additionally, allergies to apples are extremely rare. They are easy to digest and help prevent constipation, promote heart health, and control cholesterol levels.

Rice cereal

Rice cereal, many babies' first "solid" food, is easy to make at home. Bear in mind that commercial baby rice cereal is usually fortified with iron, so if you make your own, discuss your baby's iron needs with your pediatrician. Young babies can get iron from a range of foods, including breast milk, formula, meats, and dried fruit (see page 40).

¼ cup (2 oz/60 g) brown rice

**MAKES ABOUT 1 CUP
(8 FL OZ/250 ML) CEREAL**

- Put the rice in a food processor or blender and process to a fine, uniform powder, about 4 minutes.

- In a saucepan over medium-high heat, bring 1 cup (8 fl oz/250 ml) water to a simmer. Add the brown-rice powder and reduce the heat to low. Cook, whisking constantly, until the water is completely absorbed and the cereal is smooth, about 5 minutes.

- Add enough water, breast milk, or formula to thin the cereal to a consistency your baby can handle. Let cool before serving.

STORE IT Refrigerate in an airtight container for up to 3 days, or spoon individual portions into ice-cube trays or other baby-food freezer containers and freeze, covered, for up to 3 months.

MAKE MORE TO STORE Rice, barley, and millet powder are all easy to store, so grind extra to have on hand for baby's cereal. Keep the powder in an airtight container in the refrigerator until needed, then cook as directed.

Barley cereal

Vitamin-rich barley has an earthy, slightly sweet flavor and a creaminess similar to plump varieties of white rice like Arborio, but with more soluble fiber.

¼ cup (2 oz/60 g) pearl barley

MAKES ABOUT 1 CUP (8 FL OZ/250 ML) CEREAL

- Put the barley in a food processor or blender and process to a fine, uniform powder, about 5 minutes.

- In a saucepan over medium-high heat, bring 1 cup (8 fl oz/250 ml) water to a simmer. Add the barley powder and reduce the heat to low. Cook, whisking constantly, until the water is completely absorbed and the cereal is smooth, about 5 minutes.

- Add enough water, breast milk, or formula to thin the cereal to a consistency your baby can handle. Let cool before serving.

  STORE IT Refrigerate for up to 3 days, or freeze for up to 3 months.

Millet cereal

Golden, pearl-like millet has a nutty flavor and pleasant sweetness, and is similar to fluffy couscous when cooked. It is an excellent source of B vitamins, amino acids, and minerals, and is an easily digested alternative to rice.

¼ cup (2 oz/60 g) millet

MAKES ABOUT ½ CUP (4 FL OZ/125 ML) CEREAL

- Put the millet in a food processor or blender and process to a fine, uniform powder, about 2 minutes.

- In a saucepan over medium-high heat, bring 1 cup (8 fl oz/250 ml) water to a simmer. Add the millet powder and reduce the heat to low. Cook, whisking constantly, until the water is completely absorbed and the cereal is smooth, about 5 minutes.

- Add enough water, breast milk, or formula to thin the cereal to a consistency your baby can handle. Let cool before serving.

  STORE IT Refrigerate for up to 3 days, or freeze for up to 3 months.

6 MONTHS

Sweet pea puree

A naturally high sugar content makes nutritious green sweet peas an early favorite with baby, and they cook readily into a silky-smooth puree. Frozen peas are a great alternative to fresh peas in season, as they're frozen at their peak.

2 cups (10 oz/315 g) peas, fresh or frozen

MAKES ABOUT 1½ CUPS (12 FL OZ/375 ML) PUREE

- Pour water into a saucepan to a depth of 1 inch (2.5 cm). Put the peas in a steamer basket and put the basket in the saucepan. Bring to a boil over high heat. Cover and steam until the peas are bright green and tender enough to mash easily with a fork, about 5 minutes for fresh or frozen peas and about 3 minutes for thawed frozen peas.

- Remove from the heat and remove the steamer basket from the saucepan, reserving the cooking liquid. Rinse the peas under cold running water to stop the cooking. Transfer the peas to a food processor or blender and process to a smooth puree. Add enough of the reserved cooking liquid, breast milk, or formula to thin the puree to a consistency your baby can handle.

STORE IT Refrigerate in an airtight container for up to 3 days, or spoon individual portions into ice-cube trays or other baby-food freezer containers and freeze, covered, for up to 3 months.

A LITTLE VARIETY After baby has tried a number of flavors, serve up some creamy combos: Swirl together equal parts of the pea puree and Rice Cereal (page 24), or blend pea puree with a little Zucchini Puree (page 32).

6 MONTHS

Storing baby's food

Preparing homemade meals for baby doesn't have to mean spending hours in the kitchen. Cooking food in large batches and then freezing it in baby-sized portions cuts down on the overall preparation time and means that you'll always have a wide variety of healthy, homemade foods on hand for your little one.

From fridge to freezer

Freezing individual portions of food for baby will help you stretch the food further and helps save you money, with less waste from leftovers.

Once or twice a week, prepare a few different purees that you can freeze for future meals. These simple tips make storing baby's food for several months a breeze.

- After you finish preparing a recipe, let it cool to room temperature, if necessary, then transfer it to the refrigerator at once to prevent the growth of bacteria.

Formula and freezing

While the current consensus is that breast milk can be frozen without compromising nutritional value or taste, infant-formula manufacturers advise against freezing formula. While freezing won't affect the nutrient content of formula, it can cause it to separate. To make sure your baby's food tastes its best, thin it with formula after the food is defrosted rather than before freezing.

- When the food has cooled completely, set aside a small amount to keep in the refrigerator for your baby's next meal and store the remainder in the freezer.

- For easy storage and later use, spoon single-serving portions of a puree (about 2 tablespoons) into an ice cube tray or onto a baking sheet. Wrap the tray or sheet with plastic wrap and freeze completely.

- Transfer the frozen cubes or portions to a freezer-weight plastic bag and squeeze out all of the air to prevent freezer burn.

- Label and date the bag so you'll know the contents and how fresh they are.

- You can also freeze baby's purees in small baby-food freezer containers. Never freeze baby's food in glass containers as the glass can crack when food expands during freezing.

Thawing and reheating

Proper thawing and reheating ensures that baby's food is free of bacteria and safe for him to eat. Here are some tips to get you started:

- Thaw frozen baby food either in the refrigerator or the microwave. Defrosting foods at room temperature encourages bacterial growth.

- Depending on the serving size, a frozen puree will take between 12 and 24 hours to defrost in the refrigerator.

- For faster thawing, put the food in a glass container (not plastic) and defrost in the microwave, stirring the food occasionally. While using the microwave for defrosting is okay, health experts do caution against reheating meals for babies in a microwave oven as the uneven heat can cause hidden hot spots that can burn baby's mouth.

- To reheat any food for baby that needs to be slightly warmed, transfer it to a saucepan and warm gently over low heat.

- Always be sure to test the temperature of baby's food before feeding it to him.

Temperature is key

Cooking and storing baby food at the proper temperature is important for ensuring food stays fresh and free from bacteria.

When cooking meat, pork, or poultry, it's a good idea to use a meat thermometer to test for doneness. These guidelines will ensure baby's meat is cooked to the proper temperature:

- Ground (minced) meat, such as beef, lamb, and pork: 160°F (71°C)

- White and dark meat poultry: 170°F (77°C)

Home-canned foods

While freshly prepared foods that have been frozen are safe for baby, home-canned foods are not; they can contain harmful bacteria that may cause illness.

Keeping food fresh

For the most part, the foods in this book will stay fresh for up to 3 days in the refrigerator and up to 3 months in the freezer. For refrigerator storage, to keep food as fresh as possible, put it in the coldest part of the refrigerator, usually the middle shelf away from the door. For optimal taste and freshness, do not refreeze foods that have already been frozen and be sure to use thawed food within 48 hours.

- Cuts of meat, such as lamb chops or pork tenderloin: 145°F (63°C)

Bacteria are most likely to grow on food at temperatures between 40°F (4°C) and 140°F (60°C)—about the temperature of your kitchen counter, or room temperature—so, after cooking, transfer baby's food directly to your refrigerator. It's also a good idea to adjust your refrigerator and freezer to the coldest settings to ensure optimal freshness.

Pear puree

Depending on the variety, pears can vary in their firmness and their cooking time. Test for doneness by piercing the thickest part of a pear quarter with a sharp paring knife or a wooden skewer; if it goes in without resistance, the pears are done.

4 ripe pears, about 2 lb (1 kg) total weight, quartered and cored

MAKES ABOUT 2 CUPS (16 FL OZ/500 ML) PUREE

- Pour water into a large saucepan to a depth of 1 inch (2.5 cm). Put the pears in a steamer basket and put the basket in the saucepan. Bring to a boil over high heat. Cover and steam until the pears are very tender, 7–10 minutes.

- Remove from the heat and remove the steamer basket from the saucepan, reserving the cooking liquid. Let the pears cool, then remove and discard the skins. Transfer the pears to a food processor or blender and process to a smooth puree. Add enough of the reserved cooking liquid, breast milk, or formula to thin the puree to a consistency your baby can handle.

STORE IT Refrigerate in an airtight container for up to 3 days, or spoon individual portions into ice-cube trays or other baby-food freezer containers and freeze, covered, for up to 3 months. (Some slight discoloration may occur during storage.)

A LITTLE VARIETY Sweet but mild, pear puree is a good candidate for combining with single-grain cereals as baby gets older. When baby is ready to try meats, pear puree is delicious stirred into finely chopped pork or chicken (see Chapter 3).

Zucchini puree

With its mild flavor and tender texture, zucchini is a natural and nutritious first food for baby. The thin skin makes it easy to prepare and easily digestible. Feel free to substitute other summer squashes, such as yellow squash or pattypan.

2 medium zucchini (courgettes) or summer squash, about 8 oz (250 g) total weight

MAKES ABOUT 1½ CUPS (12 FL OZ/375 ML) PUREE

- Trim the zucchini and cut into rounds about 1 inch (2.5 cm) thick. Pour water into a saucepan to a depth of about 1 inch (2.5 cm). Put the zucchini rounds in a steamer basket and put the basket in the saucepan. Bring to a boil over high heat. Cover and steam until tender, about 7 minutes.

- Remove from the heat and remove the steamer basket from the saucepan, reserving the cooking liquid. Rinse the cooked zucchini under cold running water to stop the cooking. Transfer the zucchini to a food processor or blender and process to a smooth puree. If necessary, add enough of the reserved cooking liquid, breast milk, or formula to thin the puree to a consistency your baby can handle.

STORE IT Refrigerate in an airtight container for up to 3 days, or spoon individual portions into ice-cube trays or other baby-food freezer containers and freeze, covered, for up to 3 months.

FOODS TO GROW ON Since baby will eat the peel, make sure to choose organic zucchini and summer squashes. These summer vegetables are especially sweet and delicious when purchased in season at a farmers' market.

6 MONTHS

Sweet potato puree

Famously popular with both babies and kids—and chock-full of both vitamin A and fiber—sweet potatoes offer a balance of sweetness, earthiness, and soft toothsome texture. Make this puree with any of the colorful varieties of sweet potato or yams.

2 sweet potatoes or yams, about 1½ lb (750 g) total weight, scrubbed

MAKES ABOUT 2 CUPS (16 FL OZ/500 ML) PUREE

- Preheat the oven to 400°F (200°C). Prick each potato in several places with a fork and place on a baking sheet. Bake until the skins are wrinkled and the flesh is very tender, 45–60 minutes. Remove from the oven and let cool.

- Cut the potatoes in half lengthwise. Using a large metal spoon, scoop out the flesh and transfer to a food processor or blender. Discard the skins. Process to a smooth puree. Add enough water, breast milk, or formula to thin the puree to a consistency your baby can handle.

  STORE IT Refrigerate in an airtight container for up to 3 days, or spoon individual portions into ice-cube trays or other baby-food freezer containers and freeze, covered, for up to 3 months.

> **A LITTLE VARIETY** As your baby gets older and can eat thicker purees, mash part or all of the potato with a fork, leaving some chunks for texture. You can also use this same method for white-fleshed Russet potatoes, a more savory but equally pleasing puree. When baby is ready to try meats, this sweet and creamy puree is a natural alongside Turkey for Baby (page 66) and Pork for Baby (page 96).

6 MONTHS

Butternut squash puree

Use this recipe for any hard winter squash such as butternut or acorn, and for cooking pumpkins such as Sugar Pie. Roasting brings out the natural sweetness of squashes, and their bright-colored flesh, packed with vitamins and beta-carotene, whips readily into a light, smooth puree just right for baby.

1 small butternut or other winter squash, or pumpkin, about 1¼ lb (625 g)

MAKES ABOUT 2½ CUPS (20 FL OZ/625 ML) PUREE

- Preheat the oven to 375°F (190°C). Using a heavy, sharp knife, cut the squash in half lengthwise. Using a large metal spoon, scrape out the seeds and fibrous strings from the cavities and discard.

- Put the squash halves, cut side down, in a shallow baking dish. Pour water into the pan to come ¼ inch (6 mm) up the sides of the squash. Roast until very tender, 45–60 minutes. Remove from the oven and let cool.

- Using the spoon, scoop out the flesh of the squash and transfer to a food processor or blender. Discard the skins. Process to a smooth puree. Add enough water, breast milk, or formula to thin the puree to a consistency your baby can handle.

STORE IT Refrigerate in an airtight container for up to 3 days, or spoon individual portions into ice-cube trays or other baby-food freezer containers and freeze, covered, for up to 3 months.

A LITTLE VARIETY Prepare extra squash puree to make a quick and easy soup the whole family, including baby, can enjoy. Simply add enough Veggie Stock (page 53) to make a creamy, souplike version. Blend in a little bit of Applesauce (page 22) and a sprinkle of nutmeg for flavor.

6 MONTHS

Creamy avocado puree

Mild, creamy avocados are a great early food for baby. A ripe avocado requires little preparation, ready to eat by just peeling and mashing briefly. The color of avocado skins vary from green to black, but when ripe, the flesh will yield slightly to a gentle squeeze.

1 ripe avocado

MAKES ABOUT ⅓ CUP (3 FL OZ/90 ML) PUREE

- Cut the avocado in half lengthwise around the pit and twist the halves to separate. Wrap the half with the pit clinging to it in plastic wrap and reserve for another serving or another use.

- Using a spoon, scoop the flesh of the remaining avocado half into a bowl. Discard the skin. Using a fork, mash the avocado until smooth. Alternatively, transfer the avocado to a food processor or blender and process to a smooth puree. Add enough water, breast milk, or formula to thin the puree to a consistency your baby can handle.

STORE IT Avocados oxidize quickly, causing the flesh to brown and turn bitter. Try to peel only as much as you will use at one time. Wrap any unused avocado in plastic wrap and refrigerate until ready to use. With the remaining avocado half, make another serving of puree for baby—or slice it for a sandwich for yourself!

FOODS TO GROW ON Avocados are full of folate and monounsaturated fats—good for a healthy heart and for cell reproduction—and vitamin E, which is beneficial to the skin, the heart, and baby's muscles.

6 MONTHS

Banana puree

As simple to prepare as stripping off the peel, bananas are packed with nutrients, making them a perfect choice for one of baby's first fruits. If using a fork to mash the banana, be sure to eliminate all the lumps for a baby who's just getting used to solids.

1 ripe banana

MAKES ABOUT 1/2 CUP (4 FL OZ/125 ML) PUREE

- Peel the banana, cut into 3 or 4 chunks, and put in a bowl. Using a fork, mash the banana until smooth. Alternatively, transfer the banana to a food processor or blender and process to a smooth puree. Add enough water, breast milk, or formula to thin the puree to a consistency your baby can handle.

STORE IT Refrigerate the banana puree in an airtight container for up to 1 day, or spoon individual portions into an ice-cube tray or other baby-food freezer container and freeze, covered, for up to 3 months. (Some slight discoloration may occur during storage.)

FOODS TO GROW ON Famous for their potassium, which stimulates nerve impulses and muscle contractions, bananas are also high in fiber and contain good amounts of vitamin B6, vitamin C, calcium, and iron. Use fully ripe bananas to ensure that they sooth and promote digestion (unripe bananas may have the opposite effect); ripe bananas also contain more antioxidants.

6 MONTHS

Creamy Combos

Now that baby has had plenty of practice with simple, single-ingredient foods, he's ready to advance to more complex flavors and textures. This chapter is filled with delicious combinations guaranteed to tempt his appetite, which is especially important as he's increasingly eating more solid food.

Instead of basic purees, you can start to offer baby foods such as two- or three-ingredient swirls. Simple soups, stews, pilafs, and risottos, made from multiple ingredients, are also tasty ways to introduce him to thicker textures and more interesting flavors. As eating a wide variety of foods provides more of the nutrients his growing body needs, these combinations give him a nutritional boost as well.

New textures and flavors

Now that baby is regularly eating solid foods, he is ready to graduate to thicker and chunkier purees. He is also ready for more complex flavors, making this the ideal time to begin combining ingredients. At this stage, you may find that baby is drinking less breast milk or formula, wanting to eat more solid foods, and is ready for 2 meals a day.

Family meals

If you've been feeding your little one separately from the rest of the family, now is a good time to have him join in on family meals.

Even if he's not eating the same foods as everyone else, he can enjoy their company, even absorbing some of the etiquette and rhythms. While baby is not quite ready to feed himself yet, he may like holding a spoon of his own while you feed him.

Flavor explosion

By now, you've probably introduced baby to a variety of cereals, fruits, and vegetables. Combining two or three of these foods allows baby to experience a whole new set of tastes and textures, helping shape him into a more adventurous eater. The recipes in this and the previous chapter include lots of versatile purees especially suited for combining. You'll also find nourishing dishes perfect for first combinations.

When combining foods, make sure to start out by pairing ingredients that baby has already tried, in order to minimize his chances of a reaction. If he hasn't tried an ingredient, feed

The importance of iron

Iron deficiency is the most common nutrient deficiency in infants and toddlers. Because it can have lasting effects, it's important to make sure baby is getting enough iron-rich foods.

While your baby was born with his own iron supply, his reserves begin to run out around six or seven months of age. Yet, iron is especially critical now to fuel his rapid growth and his developing brain.

Feeding him iron-rich foods, such as the following, can help provide the iron your baby needs:

- Iron-fortified infant cereal
- Egg yolks
- Legumes (especially lentils)
- Red meat (lamb is high in iron), and dark-meat poultry

Also, offer baby plenty of vitamin C–rich fruits and vegetables, as these help him absorb more iron from his cereal.

If you suspect your baby isn't getting enough iron, speak to your doctor to find out if he needs a supplement.

it to him separately for 3–5 days before mixing it with anything else. Also, at this stage you can start to include butter or olive oil, a sprinkle of herbs or spices, and mild aromatics, such as leeks. Pureed meats make their debut in this chapter, with turkey and lamb.

While you will still mostly be making smooth purees, you can start trying to leave the texture as a coarse puree, or even with a little bit of chunkiness. All of this helps prepare his palate for the more complex foods he'll be eating in the coming months when you start to feed him the same foods as the rest of the family.

What's in his cup?

Now is an ideal time to introduce baby to a cup. Encouraging him to sip from a cup at mealtimes now will make weaning easier later. Because he may not be able to hold a cup himself yet, he might need your help. You may also wonder if your little one is ready for juice. The answer is: not quite yet. Right now, he still needs plenty of formula or breast milk for optimal growth, so use these to fill his cup until he's older.

Fruit 101

Fruit may be one of your baby's favorite foods. Just be sure to cook all fruits (with the exception of banana and avocado) before feeding them to baby. Cooking makes fruit easier to digest and also breaks down proteins that can potentially cause allergies at this stage.

Seasoning savvy

Your baby is enjoying many new and exciting tastes now, but there are two he can still do without: added salt and sugar. Instead, flavor his food with small amounts of the herbs and spices listed below. Make sure to try one at a time to check for any reaction. If you find some he really likes, it may prove to be helpful when trying to coax him to eat a variety of foods later. Flavorful fresh and dried herbs and spices can also start him on his way to a fine-tuned palate.

HERBS

Basil, chives, cilantro (fresh coriander), dill, marjoram, mint, oregano, parsley, rosemary, sage, tarragon, thyme

SPICES

Allspice, cardamom, cinnamon, cumin, curry powder (mild), fennel, garlic powder, ginger, nutmeg, sweet paprika, turmeric, vanilla bean

While baby can eat most fruits, you may want to hold off on feeding him citrus fruits until after his first birthday, as these can sometimes cause diaper rash. Depending on how sensitive your baby's digestive system is, peeling fruits and vegetables can also make them easier to digest.

Beet & potato swirl

This pretty autumn swirl is a comforting and delicious early combination for baby. Fresh beets are naturally sweet and a good source of folate, potassium, fiber, and disease-preventing antioxidants. Choose baby beets if possible, as they tend to be a little sweeter and less woody-textured than their larger counterparts.

1 bunch baby beets, about 1 lb (500 g) total weight, trimmed and scrubbed

1 russet potato, scrubbed

MAKES ABOUT 1½ CUPS (12 FL OZ/375 ML) PUREE

- Preheat the oven to 375°F (190°C). Place the beets in a small baking dish and add water to come ½ inch (12 mm) up the sides of the beets. Cover with aluminum foil. Prick the potato in several places with a fork and place on a small baking sheet. Place the beets and the potato in the oven and bake until very tender, 45–60 minutes. Remove from the oven and let cool.

- Peel the beets and the potato and cut into chunks, discarding the skins. Put the potato in a food processor or blender and process to a puree, adding a little water, breast milk, or formula for a smooth consistency. Transfer the potato puree to a bowl.

- Put the beets in the food processor or blender and process to a puree, again adding a little liquid for a smooth consistency. Transfer to a separate bowl. To serve, swirl together the potato and beet purees in baby's bowl.

STORE IT Refrigerate the purees separately in airtight containers for up to 3 days, or spoon individual portions into ice-cube trays or other baby-food freezer containers and freeze, covered, for up to 3 months.

A LITTLE VARIETY For another easy combination with both sweet and savory flavors, swirl the beet puree into Sweet Potato Puree (page 33) or mashed sweet potato.

Easy fruit purees

Fruit purees are among the simplest, most versatile first foods for baby. They are easy to prepare and freeze well, so you can have them on hand for quick meals or for mixing into cereal and meat or vegetable purees. High-quality frozen and dried fruits, packaged at peak ripeness, also make delicious and healthy purees.

Ripe peach puree

4 ripe peaches or nectarines, about 2 lb (1 kg) total weight, halved and pitted

MAKES ABOUT 2 CUPS (16 FL OZ/500 ML) PUREE

- Pour water into a large saucepan to a depth of 1 inch (2.5 cm). Put the peaches in a steamer basket and put the basket in the saucepan. Bring to a boil over high heat. Cover and steam until the peaches are tender but not falling apart, 4–5 minutes.

- Remove from the heat and remove the steamer basket from the saucepan. Let the peaches cool, then remove and discard the skins. Transfer the peaches to a food processor or blender and process to a smooth puree.

Berry-cherry puree

1 cup (4 oz/125 g) fresh or frozen blueberries

1 cup (4 oz/125 g) fresh or frozen pitted sweet cherries

MAKES ABOUT ¾ CUP (6 FL OZ/180 ML) PUREE

- Combine the blueberries and cherries in a food processor or blender and process to a smooth puree. If desired, to remove the skins, strain the puree through a fine-mesh sieve set over a saucepan, pushing on the solids with a rubber spatula to extract as much flesh and juice as possible. Discard the skins.

- Place the puree over medium-low heat and cook, stirring often, until heated through and thickened, about 4 minutes. Remove from the heat and let cool completely before serving.

Dried fruit puree

1 cup (6 oz/185 g) dried
apricots or prunes

MAKES ABOUT 1¼ CUPS
(10 FL OZ/310 ML) PUREE

- In a saucepan over medium-high heat, combine the apricots or prunes and 1 cup (8 fl oz/250 ml) water and bring to a boil. Reduce the heat to low, cover partially, and simmer until the fruit is tender and easily pierced with a fork, about 10 minutes. Strain the fruit through a fine-mesh sieve set over a bowl, reserving the cooking liquid. Set aside to cool.

- Transfer the cooled fruit to a food processor or blender and process to a smooth puree. Add enough of the reserved cooking liquid, breast milk, or formula to thin the puree to a consistency your baby can handle.

Plum puree

6 plums, about 2 lb (1 kg) total
weight, halved and pitted

MAKES ABOUT 2 CUPS
(16 FL OZ/500 ML) PUREE

- Pour water into a large saucepan to a depth of 1 inch (2.5 cm). Put the plums in a steamer basket and put the basket in the saucepan. Bring to a boil over high heat. Cover and steam until the plums are tender but not falling apart, about 4 minutes.

- Remove from the heat and remove the steamer basket from the saucepan. Let the plums cool, then remove and discard the skins. Transfer the plums to a food processor or blender and process to a smooth puree.

MAKE MORE TO STORE Refrigerate any of these the cooled fruit purees in an airtight container for up to 3 days, or spoon individual portions into ice-cube trays or other baby-food freezer containers and freeze, covered, for up to 3 months.

7 TO 8 MONTHS

Summer fruit "smoothie"

Once baby has tried a few different fruits, you can start making your own fruit smoothies for her. Be sure to include only fruits or fruit purees you've introduced before. For a thick, creamy texture, you can freeze the banana before blending and feed the ice-cream-like mixture to baby with a spoon.

1 banana, chilled

1 nectarine

½ cup (2 oz/60 g) frozen blueberries

½ cup (4 fl oz/125 ml) apple juice, or as needed

MAKES ABOUT 1⅓ CUPS (11 FL OZ/340 ML) SMOOTHIE

- Peel and slice the banana. Peel and pit the nectarine and cut into chunks. In a blender, combine the banana, nectarine, blueberries, and ½ cup (4 fl oz/125 ml) apple juice and blend until smooth. Add more apple juice as needed to thin the puree to a consistency your baby can handle.

- If desired, to remove the skins, strain the smoothie through a fine mesh sieve set over a bowl, pushing on the solids with a rubber spatula to extract as much as possible. Discard the solids.

STORE IT Refrigerate in an airtight container for up to 3 days, or pour individual portions into ice-cube trays or other baby-food freezer containers and freeze, covered, for up to 3 months.

A LITTLE VARIETY With banana as a base to give the smoothie sweetness and body, there are myriad fruit combinations to tickle baby's tummy. Substitute Ripe Peach Puree (page 44), apricot puree (page 45), Berry-Cherry Puree (page 44), or half of a ripe pitted and peeled avocado for the nectarine and blueberries. Once you introduce your baby to yogurt, you can add ¼ cup (2 oz/60 g) plain whole-milk yogurt to the blender for a creamy treat.

Super baby foods

Right now, baby's tiny tummy can't hold a lot of food, so every bite he takes counts. You can provide the optimum energy-to-nutrition value possible by learning about and focusing on the foods loaded with the vitamins, minerals, amino acids, fats, and phytochemicals that best fuel his growing body and brain.

Meat & poultry

BEEF A top source of iron and vitamin B12 used to build new cells

CHICKEN Provides plenty of lean, high-quality protein to support baby's rapid growth

LAMB High in iron and B vitamins, as well as zinc, which promotes a strong immune system

TURKEY Loaded with selenium, which boosts baby's immune system and helps cells grow and develop; dark-meat turkey is also an excellent source of iron

Beans & legumes

DRIED BEANS (SUCH AS RED, WHITE, PINTO, CHICKPEAS/GARBANZO) An excellent source of vegetable protein

LENTILS Higher than most legumes in protein and filled with folate

SPLIT PEAS (YELLOW OR GREEN) An easy, quick-cooking way to add protein to baby's plate

Grains

BARLEY Loaded with minerals, especially selenium, which boosts baby's immune system and helps cells grow and develop

BROWN RICE Unmilled so it retains more nutrients, such as manganese, a mineral that helps baby convert protein and carbohydrates to energy

MILLET An easy-to-digest grain that provides phosphorus to help build strong bones and teeth

QUINOA Rich in protein as well as the amino acid lysine, which promotes tissue growth

Vegetables

ASPARAGUS A top source of folate, which is needed to build new cells and tissues

PUMPKINS Filled with disease-fighting plant chemicals like alpha- and beta-carotene, plus zeaxanthin and lutein for healthy eyes

SPINACH (FOR BABIES OVER 7 MONTHS) One of nature's top sources of vitamin K, as well as being bountiful in folate and other B vitamins

SWEET POTATOES Bursting with vitamins A and C

Fruits

APRICOTS Deliver beta-carotene and vitamin A for a healthy immune system

AVOCADOS An excellent source of heart-healthy monounsaturated fats and vitamin K, needed for blood clotting

BANANAS Contain the soluble fiber pectin, which regulates digestion, making baby less prone to diarrhea or constipation

BLUEBERRIES Loaded with disease-fighting antioxidants, plus vitamin C to protect against infection

PLUMS Contain lots of vitamin C, which helps baby absorb more iron

Other nutrients

While baby needs plenty of vitamins and minerals, he also needs nutrients like carbohydrates, fats, phytochemicals, and protein for development.

CARBOHYDRATES Provide fuel to give baby energy; find it in: vegetables, fruits, grains, and beans

FAT Gives energy to fuel baby's growth; up to half of baby's calories should come from fat; find it in: breast milk/formula, oils, dairy, meat, and avocado

PHYTOCHEMICALS Substances from plants that help fight disease; find it in: vegetables, fruits, grains, and beans

PROTEIN For strong bones, muscles, skin, and teeth; find it in: breast milk/formula, dairy, meat, poultry, fish, and beans

7 TO 8 MONTHS

Baby's guacamole

Avocados are high in folate and healthy fats, with a neutral flavor and creamy consistency that make them ideal as one of baby's first foods. If you use organic English (hothouse) cucumbers, which are unwaxed and have small seeds, you can skip the step of peeling and seeding them.

1 large ripe avocado

1/2 cup (2 1/2 oz/75 g) peeled and seeded cucumber

1/4 teaspoon ground cumin

MAKES ABOUT 3/4 CUP (6 FL OZ/180 ML) GUACAMOLE

- Cut the avocado in half lengthwise around the pit and twist the halves to separate. Remove and discard the pit. Using a spoon, scoop the flesh of the avocado halves into a food processor or blender, discarding the skins.

- Using the large holes of a box grater-shredder, shred the cucumber, then add it to the food processor or blender along with the cumin. Process to a smooth puree, or, depending on baby's age and chewing ability, you can leave the puree a little coarser. If necessary, add enough water, breast milk, or formula to thin the puree to a consistency your baby can handle.

STORE IT Refrigerate in an airtight container for up to 1 day. (Some discoloration may occur during storage.)

FOODS TO GROW ON Avocados are rich in mono-unsaturated fats, which help develop the brain and central nervous system. They also contain more potassium than bananas, as well as a notable dose of lutein, a natural antioxidant that promotes healthy skin and eyes. Ripe avocados are even in color and yield very slightly to a gentle squeeze. If you buy avocados hard, let them ripen at room temperature in a paper bag.

Lamb for baby

The lamb chop is a tender and lean cut, with a mild flavor and a particularly high iron content that makes it a good choice for one of baby's first meats. It is also less likely to cause an allergic reaction than chicken or beef. Try mixing the lamb with a fruit puree such as Applesauce (page 22) or Plum Puree (page 45).

7 TO 8 MONTHS

Olive oil for greasing

1 boneless lamb steak or chop, about 6 oz (185 g) and 1 inch (2.5 cm) thick, trimmed

MAKES ABOUT ¾ CUP (6 OZ/185 G) LAMB

- Preheat the oven to 400°F (200°C). Line a small roasting pan with aluminum foil. Lightly oil a roasting rack and place it in the prepared pan. Place the lamb on the rack. Roast, turning once, until opaque throughout and no longer pink, 12–14 minutes per side. Remove from the oven and let cool.

- Using a large, sharp knife, coarsely chop the lamb, then transfer to a food processor or blender and process for 1 minute. With the machine running, add ¼ cup (2 fl oz/60 ml) water. Process until smooth. The texture will be pastelike. Add enough additional water, or breast milk or formula, to thin the puree to a consistency that your baby can handle.

STORE IT Refrigerate in an airtight container for up to 2 days, or spoon individual portions into an ice-cube tray or other baby-food freezer container and freeze, covered, for up to 1 month.

FOODS TO GROW ON When buying lamb, look for organic or naturally raised meat with pink to light red meat with little fat. Trim off any excess fat (or ask the butcher to do it for you) before cooking. Cooking and then pureeing the meat breaks down its fibers and connective tissues, making it easier for baby's body to digest the lamb and absorb its rich stores of protein and iron.

Veggie stock

Once your baby has tried each of these vegetables, you can simmer them to make a simple stock for cooking his meals. This stock is an easy way to add vitamins and minerals to purees, rice, and cereals, with the benefit of having no added sodium. If you buy organic carrots and potatoes, scrub them well and leave the peels on.

1 sweet potato or yam, peeled and cut into chunks

1 carrot, peeled and cut into chunks

1 leek, halved lengthwise, thinly sliced crosswise, and rinsed thoroughly

2 fresh flat-leaf (Italian) parsley sprigs

MAKES ABOUT 3 CUPS (24 FL OZ/750 ML) STOCK

- In a saucepan, combine the sweet potato, carrot, leek, parsley, and 5 cups (40 fl oz/1.25 l) cold water. Bring to a boil over high heat. Reduce the heat to low, cover, and simmer gently until the vegetables are very soft and the cooking liquid is lightly flavored and colored, 35–45 minutes. Remove from the heat and let cool.

- Strain the stock into a bowl through a fine-mesh sieve. (Reserve the vegetables to puree or mash for baby.) Serve the stock lukewarm or at room temperature in a cup or bottle, and/or let cool completely and store for use in other recipes.

  STORE IT Refrigerate in an airtight container for up to 3 days, or pour into ice-cube trays or other baby-food freezer containers and freeze, covered, for up to 3 months.

FOODS TO GROW ON If you're short on time, good-quality organic broths in aseptic cartons are widely available in supermarkets and natural-food stores. Unlike homemade stock, prepared broth can be heavily salted, so read the labels carefully and choose a low-sodium broth made of ingredients you recognize. Diluting purchased broth with water can give it a milder flavor.

Red lentil & rice soup

Lentils and brown rice are a nutritious, protein-packed pairing, and lentils have the added benefit of being high in folate. You can make this soup as thick or as thin as your baby can handle. Older babies might like it with a little chicken (page 92) stirred in.

2 ¾ cups (22 fl oz/680 ml) Veggie Stock (page 53), low-sodium vegetable broth, or water

⅓ cup (2 ½ oz/75 g) brown rice

½ cup (3 ½ oz/105 g) red lentils, picked over and rinsed

MAKES ABOUT 1½ CUPS (12 FL OZ/375 ML) SOUP

In a saucepan over medium-high heat, bring the stock to a simmer. Add the rice and lentils. Reduce the heat to low, cover, and simmer gently until the rice is tender, the lentils are very soft and mash easily with a spoon, and most of the liquid is absorbed, 30–35 minutes. (The mixture will continue to absorb the liquid as it cools.) Remove from the heat and let cool slightly.

Transfer the lentil-rice mixture to a food processor or blender and process to a smooth puree. Depending on your baby's age and chewing ability, you can leave the soup a little coarser, or pulse just a few times for a chunky soup; or add enough stock, broth, or water to thin the soup to a consistency your baby can handle. Serve lukewarm or at room temperature.

STORE IT Refrigerate in an airtight container for up to 3 days, or pour into ice-cube trays or other baby-food freezer containers and freeze, covered, for up to 3 months.

A LITTLE VARIETY Look for short-grain brown rice, which cooks to a softer consistency than long grain. You can also make the soup with yellow lentils or green split peas. When baby is ready, add a pinch of ground coriander or cumin to give the soup a little more flavor.

7 TO 8 MONTHS

Split pea soup

Split peas have a savory, meaty flavor and cook into smooth purees and soups ideal for baby's early eating months. Because the peas are dried and halved, they don't need presoaking like most dried beans. The earthiness of parsnip and the familiar sweetness of apple add to the appeal of this hearty soup for baby.

1 small parsnip or potato, about 4 oz (125 g), peeled

1 sweet apple or ripe pear, about 8 oz (250 g), peeled and cored

1/2 cup (3 1/2 oz/105 g) split peas, picked over and rinsed

2 1/2 cups (20 fl oz/625 ml) Veggie Stock (page 53), low-sodium vegetable broth, or water, plus more as needed

MAKES ABOUT 2 1/4 CUPS (18 FL OZ/560 ML) SOUP

- Using the large holes of a box grater-shredder, shred the parsnip and the apple. In a saucepan over medium heat, combine the shredded parsnip and apple, the split peas, and the stock. Cover and simmer until the peas are very tender and no longer grainy, about 1 hour. If the peas appear to be drying out but still aren't tender, add a little more stock as needed. Remove from the heat and let cool slightly.

- Transfer the split-pea mixture to a food processor or blender and process to a smooth or chunky puree, depending on your baby's age and chewing ability. If necessary, add additional stock, broth, or water to thin the soup to a consistency your baby can handle. Serve lukewarm or at room temperature.

STORE IT Refrigerate in an airtight container for up to 3 days, or pour into ice-cube trays or other baby-food freezer containers and freeze, covered, for up to 3 months.

MAKE MORE TO STORE Split peas, parsnips, and apples are all perennial pantry items. Make a double or triple batch of this soup if your time and energy allow; it freezes beautifully, and you can serve it to the whole family. Split peas have twice as much protein and fiber as regular peas, and lentils get the same high marks—use yellow split peas or substitute any kind of lentil here, if you like.

Creamy pumpkin risotto

With its sophisticated reputation, you might not think of serving risotto to baby, but sweet, creamy risotto is a dish that baby will love. This simplified version doesn't require constant stirring, so it's easy to make and delicious enough for the whole family; just double the recipe and pass grated Parmesan cheese for the grownups.

½ cup (3½ oz/105 g) Arborio or short-grain rice

1½ cups (12 fl oz/375 ml) Veggie Stock (page 53), low-sodium vegetable broth, or water

1 teaspoon unsalted butter

½ cup (4 fl oz/125 ml) Butternut Squash Puree (page 35) or canned pumpkin puree

Pinch of grated nutmeg

MAKES ABOUT 2 CUPS (10 OZ/315 G) RISOTTO

• In a saucepan over medium high heat, combine the rice and stock and bring to a boil. Reduce the heat to low, cover, and simmer gently, stirring occasionally, until the liquid is absorbed and the rice is soft and creamy, about 20 minutes. Remove from the heat and let stand, covered, for 10 minutes.

• Stir the butter, squash puree, and nutmeg into the rice. Depending on your baby's age and chewing ability, you can transfer the risotto to a food processor or blender and process to a coarse or smooth puree. You can also add stock, broth, or water to thin the puree to a consistency your baby can handle, if necessary. Serve lukewarm or at room temperature.

STORE IT Refrigerate in an airtight container for up to 3 days, or spoon individual portions into ice-cube trays or other baby-food freezer containers and freeze, covered, for up to 3 months.

FOODS TO GROW ON Smooth-textured winter squashes like butternut and pumpkin are some of baby's favorite first vegetables. They're full of fiber and important nutrients like vitamins A and C. Buy them when you see them in abundance at the farmers' market and store them in a cool, dry place.

Spring green risotto

This easy-to-prepare risotto is chock full of tender spring vegetables rich in vitamins, minerals, fiber, and phytochemicals (which help fight disease). Short-grained risotto rice cooks to a creamy and soft consistency, which is perfect for introducing baby to texture. If you like, double the vegetable puree and freeze it for another meal.

4 asparagus spears, tough ends trimmed

1 small zucchini (courgette), cut into slices 1/4 inch (6 mm) thick

1/2 cup (2 1/2 oz/75 g) peas, fresh or frozen

1/2 cup (3 1/2 oz/105 g) Arborio or short-grain rice

1 1/2 cups (12 fl oz/375 ml) Veggie Stock (page 53), low-sodium vegetable broth, or water

1 teaspoon unsalted butter

MAKES ABOUT 2 CUPS (16 OZ/500 G) RISOTTO

- Pour water into a large saucepan to a depth of 1 inch (2.5 cm). Put the asparagus and zucchini in a steamer basket. If using fresh peas, add them to the basket now as well. Put the basket in the saucepan. Bring to a boil over high heat. Cover and steam until the vegetables are very tender, 6–8 minutes. If using frozen peas, add them after the first 5 minutes. Transfer the steamed vegetables to a food processor or blender and process to a smooth puree, adding a little water for a smooth consistency, if necessary. Set aside.

- In a saucepan over medium-high heat, combine the rice and stock and bring to a boil. Reduce the heat to low, cover, and simmer gently, stirring occasionally, until the liquid is absorbed and the rice is soft and creamy, about 20 minutes. Remove from the heat and let stand, covered, for 10 minutes.

- Stir the butter and vegetable puree into the rice. Depending on your baby's age and chewing ability, you can transfer the risotto to a food processor or blender and process to a coarse or smooth puree. You can also add stock, broth, or water to thin the puree to a consistency your baby can handle, if necessary. Serve lukewarm or at room temperature.

STORE IT Refrigerate in an airtight container for up to 3 days, or spoon individual portions into ice-cube trays or other baby-food freezer containers and freeze, covered, for up to 3 months.

Root veggie stew

This is the perfect stew for babies ready for an array of root vegetables—sweet and soft-textured, with a subtle range of tastes. Parsnips and nutmeg give it a warm, mildly spiced flavor, making it a delicious addition to Baby's Thanksgiving (page 67).

1 teaspoon olive oil

2 carrots, peeled and cut into 1-inch (2.5-cm) chunks

2 yellow potatoes, such as Yukon gold, peeled and cut into 1-inch (2.5-cm) chunks

1 parsnip, peeled and cut into 1-inch (2.5-cm) chunks

1½ cups (12 fl oz/375 ml) Veggie Stock (page 53), low-sodium vegetable broth, or water

Pinch of grated nutmeg

MAKES ABOUT 2 CUPS (16 OZ/500 G) STEW

In a saucepan over medium-high heat, warm the olive oil. Add the carrots, potatoes, and parsnip chunks and cook, stirring often, until the parsnips and potatoes begin to turn golden, about 5 minutes. Add the stock and nutmeg and bring to a boil. Reduce the heat to medium, cover, and simmer gently until the vegetables are very tender, 25–30 minutes.

Transfer the vegetable mixture to a food processor or blender and process to a smooth puree. Depending on your baby's age and chewing ability, you can leave the stew a little coarser, or pulse just a few times for a chunky stew; or add enough stock, broth, or water to thin the puree to a consistency your baby can handle. Serve lukewarm or at room temperature.

STORE IT Refrigerate in an airtight container for up to 3 days, or spoon into ice-cube trays or other baby-food freezer containers and freeze, covered, for up to 3 months.

FOODS TO GROW ON The deeper the color of its flesh, the more healthy antioxidants a potato contains. Yellow potatoes like Yukon gold and Yellow Finn are therefore a good choice for baby—and they have the added advantage of easily whipping into an exceptionally creamy mash.

7 TO 8 MONTHS

Broccoli-cauliflower swirl

This creamy green and white puree of broccoli and cauliflower is packed with vitamins, minerals, and antioxidants. And because these ingredients are popular with babies and toddlers, this nutritious dish is certain to become a favorite. To dress it up a little, try it with a little butter and grated Parmesan cheese mixed in.

1 cup (4 oz/125 g) chopped broccoli florets

1 cup (4 oz/125 g) chopped cauliflower

MAKES ABOUT 2 CUPS (16 FL OZ/500 ML) PUREE

- Bring a saucepan three-fourths full of water to a boil over high heat. Add the cauliflower and cook until tender, 10–12 minutes. Using a slotted spoon, transfer the cauliflower to a bowl. Add the broccoli to the boiling water and cook until tender, 5–9 minutes. Drain, reserving some of the cooking liquid.

- Put the cauliflower in a food processor or blender and process to a puree, adding a little of the reserved cooking liquid for a smooth consistency, if necessary. Transfer to a bowl. Put the broccoli in the food processor or blender and process to a puree, again adding a little of the cooking liquid, if necessary. Transfer to a separate bowl. To serve, swirl together the cauliflower and broccoli purees in baby's bowl.

TO STORE Refrigerate in an airtight container for up to 3 days, or spoon into ice-cube trays or other baby-food freezer containers and freeze, covered, for up to 3 months.

A LITTLE VARIETY When baby is old enough for finger foods, cut the broccoli and cauliflower into little florets just right for practicing picking things up. Be sure to trim any stems too thick for small mouths to manage. Boil or steam until tender and toss some of each together in the serving bowl with butter and Parmesan for a colorful, tasty mix.

Baby's green bean casserole

With their earthy aromas and soft texture, mushrooms and green beans appeal to baby early in his first year of eating. Mushrooms are sometimes overlooked for their healthy qualities, which include a store of the B vitamins, riboflavin and niacin; likewise leeks, which among other powers, aid the balance of cholesterol levels.

A small handful of green beans (about 2 oz/60 g), trimmed

2 teaspoons olive oil

1 tablespoon minced leek, white parts only

2 oz (60 g) white mushrooms, brushed clean and finely diced (about ¾ cup)

⅓ cup (2½ oz/75 g) pearl barley

1½ cups (12 fl oz/375 ml) Veggie Stock (page 53), low-sodium vegetable broth, or water

¼ teaspoon dried thyme

MAKES ABOUT 1½ CUPS (12 OZ/375 G) CASSEROLE

- Pour water into a saucepan to a depth of 1 inch (2.5 cm). Put the beans in a steamer basket and put the basket in the saucepan. Bring to a boil over high heat. Cover and steam until the beans are tender, about 5 minutes. Remove from the heat and remove the steamer basket from the saucepan. Transfer the beans to a cutting board, chop coarsely, and set aside.

- In a saucepan over medium-high heat, warm the olive oil. Add the leek and mushrooms and sauté until the mushrooms soften and release their juices, 3–5 minutes. Add the barley and stir to coat with the oil and juices, about 1 minute. Add the stock and thyme and bring to a simmer. Reduce the heat to low, cover, and simmer gently until the barley is tender and most of the liquid is absorbed, 35–40 minutes.

- Stir the green beans into the barley mixture. Transfer the mixture to a food processor or blender and process to a smooth puree. Depending on your baby's age and chewing ability, you can leave the puree a little coarser, or pulse just a few times for a chunky bean casserole; or add enough stock, broth, or water to thin the puree to a consistency your baby can handle. Serve lukewarm or at room temperature.

STORE IT Refrigerate in an airtight container for up to 3 days, or spoon into ice-cube trays or other baby-food freezer containers and freeze, covered, for up to 3 months.

7 TO 8 MONTHS

Beet, squash & quinoa

Quinoa is a mild-flavored, grain-like seed that hails from South America and supplies a complete protein. It cooks into soft, round pearls with a pleasant chewiness in the center, making it a nice alternative to rice in vegetable dishes like this one. Look for it in the health-food aisle or in the bulk section of most well-stocked supermarkets.

¼ butternut or other winter squash, about 4 oz (125 g), seeded

2–3 baby beets, about 4 oz (125 g) total weight, trimmed and scrubbed

½ cup (4 oz/125 g) quinoa

2 teaspoons olive oil

1¼ cups (10 fl oz/310 ml) Veggie Stock (page 53), low-sodium vegetable broth, or water

MAKES ABOUT 2 CUPS
(16 OZ/500 G)

- Preheat the oven to 375°F (190°C). Put the squash, cut side down, in a shallow baking dish and add water to come ¼ inch (6 mm) up the sides of the squash. Put the beets in another baking dish and add water to come ½ inch (12 mm) up the sides of the beets. Cover each dish tightly with aluminum foil and roast until the squash and beets are very tender, 45–60 minutes. Remove from the oven and let cool. Scoop out the flesh of the squash and transfer to a food processor or blender, discarding the skin. Process to a smooth puree. Add enough water to thin the puree to a consistency your baby can handle. Transfer to a bowl and set aside. Repeat to peel and puree the beets and set aside.

- Rinse the quinoa under cold running water and drain well. In a saucepan over medium-high heat, warm the olive oil. Add the quinoa, stir to coat with oil, then add the stock and bring to a boil. Reduce the heat to medium-low, cover, and simmer until the liquid is absorbed and the grains are soft, about 20 minutes. Remove from the heat and let stand, covered, for 5 minutes.

- Fluff the quinoa with a fork and swirl in the vegetable purees. Depending on your baby's age and chewing ability, you can return the mixture to the food processor or blender and process to a coarse or smooth puree.

STORE IT Refrigerate in an airtight container for up to 3 days, or spoon into ice-cube trays or other baby-food freezer containers and freeze, covered, for up to 3 months.

Turkey for baby

Turkey is a great choice for one of baby's first meats; it's lean, full of B vitamins and protein, has a mild flavor, and is easy to digest. Starting with ground turkey introduces baby to the flavor of meat with a texture similar to pureed fruits or vegetables.

½ lb (250 g) ground (minced) turkey

MAKES ABOUT 1 CUP (8 OZ/250 G) TURKEY

7 TO 8 MONTHS

- In a frying pan over medium heat, combine the turkey and ¼ cup (2 fl oz/ 60 ml) water. Using a wooden spoon to break up the turkey and stirring constantly, cook until the meat is opaque throughout and no longer pink, about 4 minutes. Remove from the heat and let cool. Drain the turkey in a fine-mesh sieve set over a bowl, reserving the cooking liquid.

- Transfer the turkey to a food processor or blender and process until finely ground, about 1 minute. With the machine running, add the reserved cooking liquid, 1 tablespoon at a time, until the turkey is smooth and pastelike. Depending on your baby's age and chewing ability, add more of the cooking liquid to thin the puree to a consistency your baby can handle.

STORE IT Refrigerate in an airtight container for up to 2 days, or spoon individual portions into an ice-cube tray or other baby-food freezer container and freeze, covered, for up to 1 month.

A LITTLE VARIETY Some of baby's favorite fruit and vegetable purees, such as apricot, prune, applesauce butternut squash, and sweet potato to name a few, are delicious paired with turkey and can help to smooth the texture of the meat. Swirl 1 part fruit or vegetable puree into 2 parts turkey.

Baby's Thanksgiving

With just a little planning, baby can share the holiday feast and sample her own turkey, mashed potatoes, and cranberry-apple sauce. Set aside $1/3$ cup cranberries when making the family's cranberry sauce to make this no-sugar version for baby.

1 small russet potato, peeled and cut into 1-inch (2.5-cm) cubes

2–3 tablespoons Veggie Stock (page 53), low-sodium chicken or vegetable broth, or water

$1/2$ cup (4 oz/125 g) cooked Turkey for Baby (opposite)

$1/3$ cup ($1^1/2$ oz/45 g) fresh or thawed frozen cranberries

$1/4$ cup (2 fl oz/60 ml) apple juice

$1/2$ cup (4 fl oz/125 ml) Applesauce (page 22) or Pear Puree (page 30), plus more to taste

MAKES ABOUT 1 CUP (8 OZ/ 250 G) TURKEY-POTATO MIXTURE AND $1/2$ CUP (4 FL OZ/125 ML) CRANBERRY-APPLE SAUCE

- Bring a saucepan three-fourths full of water to a boil over high heat. Add the potato and cook until tender, 10–12 minutes. Drain, then transfer the potato to a food processor or blender and process to a puree, adding a little stock for a smooth consistency. Add the turkey, and process until well combined, adding more stock as needed to make a creamy mixture.

- In saucepan over high heat, combine the cranberries and apple juice and bring to a boil. Reduce the heat to medium-low and cook, stirring often, until the cranberries burst and the mixture thickens, about 5 minutes. Strain the mixture through a fine-mesh sieve set over a bowl, pushing on the solids with a rubber spatula to extract as much of the puree as possible. Discard the solids. In a bowl, stir together the cranberry puree and the applesauce. Taste for sweetness, adding more applesauce if it seems too tart.

- To serve, spoon some of the cranberry-apple sauce alongside some of the turkey-potato mixture in baby's dish.

STORE IT Refrigerate the cranberry-apple and turkey-potato mixtures separately in airtight containers for up to 2 days, or spoon individual portions into ice-cube trays or other baby-food freezer containers and freeze, covered, for up to 1 month.

Apricot & coconut milk rice pudding

This creamy rice pudding has a texture baby will love, while introducing new, floral flavors. All of its sweetness comes naturally, from nutrient-rich coconut milk, fluffy jasmine rice, and a colorful splash of fresh apricot puree. You can substitute nearly any fruit puree, such as Plum Puree (page 45) or Banana Puree (page 37), for the apricot.

½ cup (3½ oz/105 g) jasmine rice

¾ cup (6 fl oz/180 ml) coconut milk, plus more as needed

½ cup (3 oz/90 g) dried apricots

MAKES ABOUT 2½ CUPS
(20 FL OZ/625 ML) PUDDING

- In a saucepan over medium-high heat, combine the rice and 1 cup (8 fl oz/250 ml) water and bring to a boil. Reduce the heat to low, cover, and simmer gently, stirring occasionally, until the liquid is absorbed and the rice is soft and creamy, 15–20 minutes. Remove from the heat and stir in the ¾ cup (6 fl oz/180 ml) coconut milk. Set aside to cool.

- Meanwhile, in another saucepan over medium-high heat, combine the apricots and ½ cup (4 fl oz/125 ml) water and bring to a boil. Reduce the heat to low, cover partially, and simmer until the fruit is tender, about 10 minutes. Strain the fruit through a fine-mesh sieve set over a bowl, reserving the cooking liquid. Set aside to cool.

- Transfer the cooled fruit to a food processor or blender and process to a smooth puree. Add enough of the reserved cooking liquid to thin the puree to a consistency your baby can handle.

- Transfer the cooled rice mixture to the food processor or blender and process until smooth and creamy. The mixture will be thick, so add more coconut milk or reserved apricot-cooking water as needed to achieve a creamy consistency or a consistency your baby can handle. Spoon some of the rice pudding into a bowl and top with a spoonful of apricot puree.

STORE IT Refrigerate the apricot puree and rice pudding separately in airtight containers for up to 3 days, or spoon individual portions into ice-cube trays or other baby-food freezer containers and freeze, covered, for up to 3 months.

7 TO 8 MONTHS

Super chunky

Suddenly, baby will be more interested in becoming an active participant at meal times. Physically, she's ready for thicker, chunkier foods. She's also developing skills to feed herself such as picking up small pieces of food and then putting them in her mouth. As a result, she needs new foods to practice on. This chapter gives guidance on introducing baby to heartier textures and finger foods.

Now that her digestive system is more mature and less prone to food allergies, this chapter also focuses on new foods to introduce. These allow baby to explore the world of self-feeding with mashed and chopped versions of many of the same foods the rest of the family is eating.

Making strides

Now that baby is between 9 and 11 months, you may notice that her appetite is growing and that she's eating more solid foods. At this stage, most babies eat 3 meals a day, although some may need an additional snack to keep them satisfied.

New skills, new foods

Even though baby may not have sprouted any teeth yet, she can use her gums to mash soft foods. That means she's ready for thicker and chunkier textures, so get ready for more mashing with a fork or potato masher and less pureeing. You can also pulse foods—rather than pureeing them—in your food processor or blender to achieve a chunkier consistency.

At first, you can ease the transition by mixing mashed food or coarse or chunky purees with a small amount of smoothly pureed food. Little by little, as she adjusts to thicker textures, you can slowly start to subtract the amount of smooth food and favor chunkier options. Now is also the time to offer baby some soft "big kid" foods such as oatmeal, shredded cheese, and soft, cooked vegetables for dipping.

During this stage you are likely to discover that your baby has mastered a new skill: picking up small objects with her thumb and index finger. Going forward, she'll use this skill, called the "pincer grip," to feed herself finger foods. Putting pieces of dry unsweetened cereal, soft cubes of ripe banana or avocado, well-cooked ground meat, or teething crackers on her plate will give her plenty of practice (see pages 80–81).

Little miss independent

Just a few months ago, your baby completely relied on you to feed her. Now, she's able to help a bit. In addition to learning to feed herself finger foods, she may be able to hold her own spoon. She may also hold her own cup with two hands and drink from it—with a few spills.

One of the biggest surprises right now is that baby may want to start feeding herself. Signs that she craves more involvement include grabbing the spoon or making a fuss when you try to feed her. If your little one wants to feed herself, go ahead and let her. Things may get messy (try the time-tested technique of a towel

Keep it social

Meal times aren't just about food. They're also about conversation and communication.

Talk to your baby during meals and teach her the names of the foods she's eating and the utensils she's using. By pointing out the different colors on her plate, you can help her learn her colors.

under her high chair), but giving baby a sense of control over what she eats now will make her a more flexible eater later. It will also help her learn to regulate how much she eats. While she may want to feed herself everything, you may still need to step in and lend a helping hand with runny foods such as cereal or soup.

Follow the leader

Even though baby may be holding her own spoon and starting to drink from her own cup, she still looks to you for guidance, watching your reactions to how and how much she eats. Let her know that it's okay for her to experiment with feeding herself independently.

A parent who is calm and relaxed at meal and snack times is far more likely to have an enthusiastic, adventurous eater than a parent who is continually trying to get baby to eat all of her vegetables. If baby makes a mess while eating or turns her nose up at certain foods, react with calm indifference. Your relaxed attitude will let her know that you are at ease with her taking the lead.

What she's eating now

Because she's developed new feeding skills and is less prone to certain food allergies now, baby is ready for new foods such as whole-milk yogurt, ricotta cheese, and small-curd cottage cheese, wheat (such as whole-grain breads spread with veggie or fruit puree and cut into small bites),

9 TO 11 MONTHS

Safety sense

Even though baby is now branching out and trying a lot of new foods, there are a few she's still not ready for yet. Be sure to hold off giving her sticky foods like peanut butter or raisins, which can cause choking. And remember, even though she is now starting to feed herself, she still needs your supervision whenever she's eating.

and cooked egg yolk (hard-boiled and finely mashed, or scrambled). Egg whites are still restricted at this age, however, as doctors recommend a no-egg-white rule during the first year due to common egg allergies.

Dishes can now feature more aromatic additions, including onions, garlic, and ginger, and a more ambitious mix of herbs and spices, such as cumin and sweet paprika. Chicken and pork enter the meat menu; just be sure to cook any pieces of meat until they are opaque throughout, with no pinkness in the middle.

You can also start to give baby 100-percent fruit juice; however, continue to hold off on citrus. Be sure to limit the amount of juice to $1/4$ cup (2 fl oz/60 ml) a day; more than this can cause diarrhea and fill her up, making her less interested in other foods. Introduce juice in a cup since you'll be weaning her from her bottle soon.

Apple-cinnamon oatmeal

Oatmeal paired with just about any fruit makes a delicious breakfast for baby. Try stirring mashed banana, Berry-Cherry Puree (page 44), prune puree (page 45), or Applesauce (page 22) into plain oatmeal. You could also substitute finely chopped ripe pears, peaches, or nectarines for the shredded apple in this simple recipe.

9 TO 11 MONTHS

1 sweet apple such as Pink Lady, McIntosh, or Gala

1 cup (3 oz/90 g) old-fashioned rolled oats

¼ teaspoon ground cinnamon

MAKES ABOUT 2 CUPS (14 OZ/440 G) OATMEAL

- Peel and core the apple. Using the large holes of a box grater-shredder, shred the apple and set aside.

- In a saucepan over high heat, bring 2 cups (16 fl oz/500 ml) water to a boil. Stir in the oats, shredded apple, and cinnamon. Return to a boil, then reduce the heat to medium-low and simmer until the oatmeal begins to thicken, about 5 minutes. Remove from the heat, cover, and let stand until thick and creamy, about 10 minutes. Add enough water, breast milk, or formula to thin the oatmeal to a consistency your baby can handle. Let cool.

STORE IT Refrigerate in an airtight container for up to 3 days. To refresh the oatmeal, stir in a few tablespoons warm water.

FOODS TO GROW ON Unlike quick oats, old-fashioned oats retain their bran and germ during processing, which means that they also retain their healthy fiber and cholesterol-fighting nutrients like selenium.

Savory brown rice

This nutritious staple is the basis for any number of baby and toddler meals. Some of the many good options for stir-ins include Applesauce (page 22), Creamy Avocado Puree (page 36), and Beet and Potato Swirl (page 42). Or try the rice alongside Root Veggie Stew (page 61) or Creamy Chicken Curry (page 93).

9 TO 11 MONTHS

1 cup (7 oz/220 g) brown rice

2 cups (16 fl oz/500 ml) Veggie Stock (page 53), low-sodium broth, or water

MAKES ABOUT 3 CUPS (15 OZ/470 G) RICE

- In a medium saucepan over high heat, combine the rice and the stock and bring to a boil. Reduce the heat to low, cover, and simmer gently until the liquid is absorbed and the rice is tender, about 50 minutes. Remove from the heat and let stand, covered, for about 5 minutes.

- Depending on your baby's age and chewing ability, you can transfer the rice to a food processor or blender, along with ¼ cup (2 fl oz/60 ml) water to prevent sticking, and process to a smooth or coarse puree. The rice may still be very sticky, so blend with a few tablespoons of fruit or vegetable puree to smooth it out (see note above), if you like.

STORE IT Refrigerate in an airtight container for up to 3 days, or spoon individual portions into ice-cube trays or other baby-food freezer containers and freeze, covered, for up to 3 months.

FOODS TO GROW ON Brown rice—a more nutritious choice than white—has had only the outermost hulls removed from the grains, leaving them full of fiber, vitamins, and nutrients. Look for short-grain brown rice, which cooks to a softer texture than long grain.

Creamy avocado-egg spread

While pediatricians recommend that baby avoid egg whites during the first year, he can still get the benefit of their high protein and iron content by eating the yolk. Mashed with avocado, the cooked yolks add fluffy body and rich flavor to a mild spread that's perfect for bread or toast.

2 large eggs

2 tablespoons plain whole-milk yogurt

½ ripe avocado

1 slice whole-wheat (wholemeal) bread (optional), for serving

MAKES ABOUT ½ CUP (4 OZ/125 G) SPREAD

● Put the eggs in a small saucepan and add water to cover by 1 inch (2.5 cm). Bring to a boil over medium-high heat. As soon as the water reaches a boil, remove from the heat, cover the pan, and let stand for 14 minutes. Drain and rinse the eggs under cold running water to stop the cooking. Peel the eggs, then slice in half and remove the yolks. Reserve the egg whites for another use or discard.

● In a small bowl, combine the yolks, yogurt, and avocado and mash with a fork with until smooth. Spread some of the mixture onto the bread slice and cut into small pieces or strips for baby to serve himself.

STORE IT Refrigerate in an airtight container for up to 1 day, or spoon individual portions into ice-cube trays or other baby-food freezer containers and freeze, covered, for up to 3 months. (Some discoloration may occur during storage.)

ALLERGY ALERT If you haven't yet introduced wheat to your baby, the wide selection of gluten-free breads available in most well-stocked supermarkets provide excellent alternatives. These breads are made from grains other than wheat, such as rye, barley, and millet. Ask your pediatrician which are right for your baby's age.

Egg yolk & asparagus omelet

This tiny omelet is a great way for baby to get the benefit of protein and iron-rich egg yolks, and to be able to enjoy an egg dish at the table with the rest of the family. Feel free to substitute a tablespoon of another finely chopped or mashed soft-cooked vegetable, such as broccoli or peas, for the asparagus.

1 asparagus spear, tough end trimmed

1 large egg yolk

2 teaspoons grated Parmesan cheese

½ teaspoon unsalted butter or olive oil

MAKES 1 MINI OMELET

- Pour water into a saucepan to a depth of 1 inch (2.5 cm). Put the asparagus in a steamer basket and put the basket in the saucepan. Bring to a boil over high heat. Cover and steam until the asparagus is tender, about 5 minutes. Remove from the heat and remove the steamer basket from the saucepan. Transfer the asparagus to a cutting board and chop very finely.

- In a small bowl, whisk together the egg yolk, asparagus, cheese, and 1 teaspoon water. Set aside.

- In a nonstick frying pan over medium-high heat, melt the butter. Pour the egg mixture into the pan and, using a spatula, scrape the edges of the egg toward the center of the pan as it sets, piling it in a circle 3–4 inches (7.5–10 cm) in diameter. When the egg is set but still moist on the surface, turn with the spatula. Cook for 1 minute longer, then transfer to a plate. Let cool slightly, then roll the omelet into a cylinder and cut into pinwheels or smaller pieces, depending on baby's age and chewing ability.

ALLERGY ALERT Eggs, especially the whites, are among the top food allergens, which is why most pediatricians advise waiting to introduce egg whites to baby until after a year. Let your pediatrician know of food allergies in your family; he or she may advise waiting to introduce yolks.

Finger foods

For the first half year (and then some) of her life, your baby is most likely happy for you to feed her when she eats. That may start to change around the age of nine months, when most babies become interested in taking a more active part in their meals. Offering her finger foods now is the ideal way to help her make the transition.

Finger-food fundamentals

The transition from soft, mashed foods to finger foods is a completely new experience for baby. Not only will she be experimenting with new tastes and textures, she'll also be developing new motor skills as well. Making baby's first experiences with finger foods as enjoyable as possible can ease the transition for both of you.

Signs your baby is ready for finger foods

The best time to begin offering your baby finger foods is when she has started practicing all the physical skills she needs to feed herself. Here are cues that she's ready:

- She can sit without your assistance.
- She is interested in feeding herself.
- She can pick up small objects using her thumb and forefinger (known as the "pincer grip").
- She can easily bring objects up to her mouth.
- She can mash food with her gums.

Start small

Start with foods that are familiar to baby. Offer her small pieces of favorite soft foods that she's already eaten mashed or pureed.

You can minimize the chances of choking by making sure each bite is small enough for her to mash with her gums or soft enough to melt in her mouth.

Offer finger foods at snack time

In the beginning, rather than feeding your baby finger foods at meal times, start off by offering one or two pieces at snack time. This will provide her with the opportunity to practice at a leisurely pace. What's more, you won't have to worry if she only takes a bite or two. If baby eats them happily, go ahead and give her more until she shows signs that she is full.

Be patient

Some babies warm up to finger foods faster than others; at first, your baby may be more interested in playing with her food than eating it. Allowing your little one to feed herself can also be messy! Rest assured that as she becomes better at self feeding, more of her food will end up in her mouth and less on the floor.

A feast for the senses

When your baby eats, taste is only part of the experience. Now that she's experimenting with finger foods, she'll become more interested in the way her food feels in her hands, its color, and its aroma. Offering her finger foods with bright colors and a variety of textures helps stimulate her senses. Allow for a little extra time at each meal to make it a pleasant experience.

Sticky little hands

A baby who is busy exploring the world from the floor often has a dirty set of hands! Now that baby is touching everything she eats, you'll want to make sure those hands are nice and clean.

Finger foods to avoid

Wait until baby is older and more adept at eating before giving her foods that are hard, sticky, or difficult to chew:

- Raisins or other dried fruit
- Whole grapes
- Cherry tomatoes or grape tomatoes
- Raw, hard vegetables and fruits like carrots, celery, and apples
- Sausages, including hot dogs
- White bread
- Popcorn
- Hard cheese

Favorite finger foods

These flavorful foods are soft enough for baby to easily mash with her gums:

- Well-cooked ground (minced) turkey, beef, or lamb
- Thin slices of deli meat such as roasted turkey breast
- Small chunks of banana, peach, nectarine, melon, mango, papaya or plum; pieces of baked apple or pear; blueberries
- Cooked pieces of regular or sweet potato, broccoli, carrots, beets, butternut squash, or asparagus sprinkled with grated Parmesan
- Scrambled eggs, finely chopped
- Pieces of pancake, waffles, or French toast, finely chopped
- Dry cereals that melt in the mouth
- Small shapes of cooked pasta or cut-up noodles, tossed with shredded Cheddar or mozzarella
- Small cubes of firm tofu, which can be dusted with dried or fresh toasted bread crumbs
- Small pieces of whole-grain toast spread with ricotta cheese

TIP Coat slippery foods like banana or ripe avocado in toasted wheat germ or crushed graham crackers to make them easier for baby to pick up.

Creamy hummus dip

In addition to the roasted pepper strips, offer this healthy chickpea spread with a variety of fun-to-hold dippers, such as tender sticks of cooked carrot or zucchini and small strips of toasted whole-wheat (wholemeal) bread or pita. Chickpeas, the main ingredient in hummus, are exceptionally nutritious and packed with protein and fiber.

9 TO 11 MONTHS

1 red bell pepper (capsicum)

1 can (15 oz/470 g) cooked low-sodium chickpeas (garbanzo beans), rinsed and drained

1/3 cup (2 1/2 oz/75 g) plain whole-milk yogurt

1 small clove garlic (optional)

2 tablespoons olive oil

1/2 teaspoon ground cumin

MAKES ABOUT 2 1/2 CUPS (20 OZ/625 G) HUMMUS

- Line a broiler pan with aluminum foil and preheat the broiler (grill). Place the bell pepper on the prepared pan and broil (grill), turning occasionally, until the skin is blackened all over. Transfer to a paper bag or a bowl. Close the bag tightly or cover the bowl with plastic wrap and let the pepper steam to help loosen the skin. Let stand until cool.

- When cool enough to handle, cut the pepper in half and remove and discard the seeds, stem, and blackened skin.

- In a food processor or blender, combine the chickpeas, half of the roasted pepper, the yogurt, the garlic (if using), the olive oil, and the cumin and process until smooth. Cut the other half of the bell pepper into small strips for dipping.

STORE IT Refrigerate the hummus in an airtight container for up to 1 week; refrigerate the pepper strips for up to 3 days.

MAKE MORE TO STORE It's easy to roast extra red bell peppers while the broiler is hot. Puree and freeze the roasted peppers to use in this hummus another time, to stir into ricotta or cottage cheese, or to serve along with baby's chicken (page 92) or pork (page 96).

Baby's "baked" potato

Here is a baby-friendly version of a comfort-food classic and a fun way for baby to enjoy creamy potatoes—especially appealing if the whole family is having them. Yukon gold potatoes are a good choice because their small size is perfect for little appetites.

1 Yukon gold potato, peeled and cut into 1-inch (2.5-cm) cubes

1/2 teaspoon unsalted butter, melted

1 1/2 tablespoons plain whole-milk yogurt

2 teaspoons grated Parmesan or Cheddar cheese

1 fresh chive sprig, minced (optional)

MAKES ABOUT 1/2 CUP (4 OZ/125 G) POTATO

- Bring a small saucepan three-fourths full of water to a boil over high heat. Add the potato, reduce the heat to medium, and cook until very tender, 10–12 minutes. Drain the potato thoroughly in a colander, return to the warm pan, and add the butter.

- Depending on your baby's age and chewing ability, mash the potato with a potato masher or fork until smooth or leave slightly chunky. Cool slightly, then stir in the yogurt, cheese, and chive, if using, and serve.

FOODS TO GROW ON Because of pesticide residue that can remain even after peeling, potatoes are among the vegetables that experts especially recommend buying organic, particularly for children.

Cheesy broccoli casserole

This savory dish combines some of baby's favorite tastes, including the new, gooey delights of cheese. You can cook the fillings and assemble the casseroles in advance and refrigerate until ready to bake. Make sure to cool completely before serving.

Unsalted butter for greasing

1 cup (2 oz/60 g) broccoli florets

2 teaspoons olive oil

1 tablespoon minced shallot

$\frac{1}{2}$ cup ($1\frac{1}{2}$ oz/45 g) finely chopped white mushrooms

$\frac{2}{3}$ cup ($3\frac{1}{2}$ oz/105 g) cooked Savory Brown Rice (page 76)

$\frac{1}{4}$ cup (2 fl oz/60 ml) Veggie Stock (page 53), low-sodium vegetable broth, or water

6 tablespoons ($1\frac{1}{2}$ oz/45 g) shredded white Cheddar or Monterey jack cheese

MAKES 4 MINI CASSEROLES

- Preheat the oven to 375°F (190°C). Lightly butter four $\frac{1}{2}$-cup (4–fl oz/125-ml) ramekins or custard cups.

- Pour water into a saucepan to a depth of 1 inch (2.5 cm). Put the broccoli in a steamer basket and put the basket in the saucepan. Bring to a boil over high heat. Cover and steam until the broccoli is tender, 6–8 minutes. Remove from the heat and remove the steamer basket from the saucepan. Transfer the broccoli to a cutting board and chop very finely. Set aside.

- In a frying pan over medium heat, warm the olive oil. Add the shallot and mushrooms and cook until the mushrooms start to release their juices and are tender, about 5 minutes. Remove from the heat and stir in the rice, broccoli, stock, and 3 tablespoons of the cheese. Divide the mixture evenly among the prepared ramekins and sprinkle the remaining 3 tablespoons cheese evenly over the tops.

- Bake until the cheese is melted and bubbling, 20–25 minutes. Let cool completely before serving to baby.

STORE IT Refrigerate the baked casseroles for up to 3 days or freeze, covered, for up to 3 months. Thaw in the refrigerator, then let come to room temperature before serving.

9 TO 11 MONTHS

Tofu, rice & avocado

Tofu, brown rice, and ripe avocado are earthy, mild flavors that are rich with healthful oils. These ingredients have the added advantage of being the perfect starter finger foods, letting baby practice her pincer grip and get used to feeding herself.

½ cup (4 oz/125 g) plain firm tofu, cut into small cubes

½ cup (2½ oz/75 g) cooked Savory Brown Rice (page 76)

½ ripe avocado, cut into small cubes

1 tablespoon finely chopped cilantro (fresh coriander)

MAKES 1½ CUPS
(12 OZ/375 G)

- In a bowl, combine the tofu, rice, avocado, and cilantro and toss gently to mix. If baby is interested in picking up the food with her fingers, spread a little on her highchair tray and let her pick up the pieces, helping her as needed.

- For babies not yet ready for finger foods, transfer the mixture to a food processor or blender and process to a coarse or smooth puree. You can add stock, broth, or water to thin the puree to a consistency your baby can handle, if necessary.

STORE IT Refrigerate in an airtight container for up to 3 days. (Some discoloration may occur during storage.)

ALLERGY ALERT Tofu is packed with protein and calcium, and its mild flavor and soft texture make it a favorite early food with babies. However, if you have food allergies in your family, ask your pediatrician when it's best to introduce tofu or other soy products to your baby.

9 TO 11 MONTHS

Beans, banana & quinoa

Soft, cooked black beans and chopped bananas make perfect finger foods for a baby just learning to feed himself. If you use canned beans, make sure to rinse them well. Avocado, another favorite finger food, is a yummy alternative for the banana, or for older babies, you can substitute finely chopped mango or papaya.

9 TO 11 MONTHS

½ cup (4 oz/125 g) quinoa

1 cup (7 oz/220 g) cooked low-sodium black beans, rinsed and drained

¼ banana, finely chopped

MAKES ABOUT 2 CUPS (16 OZ/500 G)

- Rinse the quinoa under cold running water and drain well. In a small saucepan, combine the quinoa and 1 cup (8 fl oz/250 ml) water and bring to a boil over high heat. Reduce the heat to low, cover, and simmer gently until the liquid is absorbed and the grains are soft and translucent, about 20 minutes. Let stand, covered, for 10 minutes.

- Meanwhile, in another small saucepan, heat the beans over medium heat and mash some or all of them with a fork to a consistency your baby can handle. Fluff the quinoa with the fork and stir in the beans. Spoon the quinoa mixture onto a plate, top with the banana, and serve lukewarm or at room temperature.

STORE IT Refrigerate the bean-quinoa mixture in an airtight container for up to 3 days, or freeze for up to 3 months. Top with the banana just before serving.

FOODS TO GROW ON Often touted as a highly nutritious grain, quinoa is actually a seed native to South America. It is high in protein and amino acids, and cooks to a soft fluffy texture that is pleasing for baby. It also makes a good substitute for brown rice.

Cauliflower & brown rice gratin

Creamy cauliflower puree and nutty whole-grain brown rice pair up in this classic savory dish. Cauliflower belongs to the cruciferous family of vegetables, noted for their vitamins, fiber, and disease-fighting phytochemicals. Make sure to let the gratins cool completely so eager little fingers don't get burned.

Unsalted butter for greasing

1 cup (2 oz/60 g) cauliflower florets

$1/2$ cup (2 oz/60 g) grated Parmesan cheese

Pinch of grated nutmeg

1 cup (5 oz/155 g) cooked Savory Brown Rice (page 76)

4 tablespoons (2 fl oz/60 ml) Veggie Stock (page 53), low-sodium vegetable broth, or water

MAKES 4 MINI GRATINS

- Preheat the oven to 375°F (190°C). Lightly butter four $1/2$-cup (4–fl oz/125-ml) ramekins or custard cups.

- Pour water into a saucepan to a depth of 1 inch (2.5 cm). Put the cauliflower in a steamer basket and put the basket in the saucepan. Bring to a boil over high heat. Cover and steam until the cauliflower is tender, 6–8 minutes. Remove from the heat and remove the steamer basket from the saucepan. Transfer the cauliflower to a food processor or blender and process to a smooth puree, adding a little water for a smooth consistency, if necessary. Stir $1/4$ cup (1 oz/30 g) of the cheese and the nutmeg into the cauliflower puree. Set aside.

- Divide the rice evenly among the prepared ramekins, patting it into the bottoms. Drizzle each with 1 tablespoon of the stock. Spoon the cauliflower puree into each ramekin, dividing it evenly and smoothing the top to cover the rice. Top each ramekin with 1 tablespoon of the remaining cheese.

- Bake until the tops are golden brown, about 20 minutes. Let cool completely before serving to baby.

STORE IT Refrigerate the baked gratins for up to 3 days or freeze, covered, for up to 3 months. Thaw in the refrigerator, then let come to room temperature before serving.

Indian-spiced lentil stew

Red and green lentils are among the easiest legumes to prepare, since they don't need to be soaked and become tender after just 20 minutes of cooking time. Garlic and aromatic spices liven up this stew and help expand baby's flavor palate. Serve the stew by itself, or with a little Savory Brown Rice (page 76).

1 tablespoon olive oil

1 carrot, peeled and finely chopped

1 medium red potato, peeled and finely chopped

1/4 yellow onion, finely chopped

1 small clove garlic, minced

1/4 teaspoon ground coriander

1/4 teaspoon ground cumin

1/4 teaspoon ground cinnamon

1/3 cup (2 1/2 oz/75 g) red lentils, picked over and rinsed

2 cups (16 fl oz/500 ml) Veggie Stock (page 53), low-sodium vegetable broth, or water, plus more as needed

MAKES ABOUT 3 CUPS (24 OZ/750 G) STEW

- In a saucepan over medium-high heat, warm the olive oil. Add the carrot, potato, onion, and garlic and sauté until the vegetables start to sweat, about 5 minutes. Add the coriander, cumin, and cinnamon and stir to mix well, then add the lentils and the stock. Stir to combine. Bring to a boil, then reduce the heat to low, cover, and simmer gently until the vegetables and lentils are very tender, about 20 minutes.

- Depending on your baby's age and chewing ability, serve whole or use a fork to mash the stew to a consistency your baby can handle, or transfer the stew to a food processor or blender and process to a coarse or smooth puree, adding more stock or water as needed. Let cool slightly, then serve.

STORE IT Refrigerate in an airtight container for up to 3 days, or spoon individual portions into ice-cube trays or other baby-food freezer containers and freeze, covered, for up to 3 months.

FOODS TO GROW ON Lentils are the nutrition stars of the legume family—they have twice as much protein as many of their cousins, and also provide iron, phosphorus, calcium, and B vitamins such as niacin and folate.

Chicken for baby

When baby is first introduced to meats, mixing them with a fruit puree such as Plum Puree (page 45) or Applesauce (page 22); a vegetable puree such as mashed sweet potato (page 33) or Butternut Squash Puree (page 35); or a cooked grain such as Savory Brown Rice (page 76), can make the texture more appealing.

Olive oil for greasing

½ lb (250 g) boneless, skinless chicken thighs or breasts

MAKES ABOUT 1¼ CUPS (8 OZ/250 G) CHICKEN

- Preheat the oven to 400°F (200°C). Line a small roasting pan with aluminum foil. Lightly oil a roasting rack and place it in the prepared pan. Place the chicken on the rack and bake, turning once about halfway through the baking time, until opaque throughout and no longer pink in the center, about 30 minutes. Remove from the oven and let cool.

- Transfer the chicken to a cutting board and, using a sharp knife, cut the chicken across the grain into thin slices, then mince the slices into very small pieces. Depending on your baby's age and chewing ability, you can transfer the chicken to a food processor or blender and pulse just until the texture resembles small crumbs; add a little water if needed to moisten.

STORE IT Refrigerate in an airtight container for up to 2 days, or spoon individual portions into ice-cube trays or other baby-food freezer containers and freeze, covered, for up to 1 month.

FOODS TO GROW ON When buying chicken, choose meat that has been raised naturally or organically, free of hormones and antibiotics. As baby becomes more adept at chewing and mastering her pincer grip, cut the chicken into small pieces instead of mincing.

Creamy chicken curry

This mildly spiced dish eases baby into the world of fragrant garlic and sweet, spicy ginger. Coconut milk typically comes in 14–fl oz (430-ml) cans, so make an extra large batch of curry to store, or freeze the remainder of the can for making Veggie Curry (page 118) or Apricot and Coconut Milk Rice Pudding (page 69).

½ cup (3 oz/90 g) green beans, trimmed

½ cup (3 oz/90 g) Chicken for Baby (opposite)

1 teaspoon canola oil

1 green (spring) onion, white and pale green parts only, finely chopped

1 small clove garlic, minced

1 teaspoon peeled and grated fresh ginger

½ cup (4 fl oz/125 ml) coconut milk

½ cup (4 fl oz/125 ml) Veggie Stock (page 53) or low-sodium vegetable or chicken broth

1 teaspoon finely chopped fresh basil

Savory Brown Rice (page 76) or cooked brown rice for serving

MAKES ABOUT 2½ CUPS (20 OZ/625 G) CURRY

- Pour water into a small saucepan to a depth of 1 inch (2.5 cm). Put the beans in a steamer basket and put the basket in the saucepan. Bring to a boil over high heat. Cover and steam until the beans are tender, about 5 minutes. Remove from the heat and remove the steamer basket from the saucepan. Transfer the beans to a cutting board, chop finely, and set aside.

- Prepare the chicken as directed, but chop finely (do not puree in the food processor or blender). In a saucepan over medium-low heat, warm the oil. Add the green onion and sauté just until the onion wilts, about 2 minutes. Stir in the garlic and ginger and cook, stirring, for 1 minute.

- Stir in the coconut milk and stock, raise the heat to medium-high, and bring to a boil. Reduce the heat to low and add the green beans, chicken, and basil. Simmer, covered, until the sauce has thickened slightly and the chicken is warmed through, about 2 minutes. Remove from the heat and let cool. Serve lukewarm or at room temperature with the rice.

STORE IT Refrigerate in an airtight container for up to 2 days, or spoon individual portions into ice-cube trays or other baby-food freezer containers and freeze, covered, for up to 1 month.

9 TO 11 MONTHS

Baby's chicken chili

Protein-rich and full of fiber, beans are a great food for baby. They're also fun to try to pick up with little fingers—good practice for her pincer grip. This mildly spiced chicken-and-bean "chili" is a nutritious way to enjoy this classic dish, made especially for baby. A pinch of mild chili powder can be added for older toddlers.

1 cup (7 oz/220 g) cooked low-sodium black or pinto beans, rinsed and drained

¼ cup (2 fl oz/60 ml) Veggie Stock (page 53), low-sodium vegetable broth, or water

¼ teaspoon ground cumin

⅛ teaspoon paprika

½ cup (3 oz/90 g) Chicken for Baby (page 92)

1½ tablespoons finely chopped fresh cilantro (fresh coriander)

MAKES 1½ CUPS
(12 OZ/375 G) CHILI

- In a saucepan over high heat, combine the beans, stock, cumin, and paprika. Bring to a boil, then reduce the heat to medium-low and simmer, stirring occasionally, until the beans are heated through and the sauce has thickened slightly, 5–8 minutes.

- Depending on your baby's age and chewing ability, use a fork to mash some or all of the beans to a consistency your baby can handle. Stir in the chicken and cilantro and serve, or transfer the chili to a food processor or blender and process to a coarse or smooth puree, adding more stock or water as needed.

STORE IT Refrigerate in an airtight container for up to 3 days, or spoon individual portions into ice-cube trays or other baby-food freezer containers and freeze, covered, for up to 1 month.

A LITTLE VARIETY When baby is old enough to eat tomatoes (see Chapter 5), add ½ cup (3 oz/90 g) finely chopped ripe tomatoes to the beans during the simmering step. The sugars and acid in tomatoes will brighten the flavors of the juices and add a shot of vitamin C.

Pork for baby

Smooth out the texture of this simple roasted pork tenderloin by combining it with a fruit puree such as Applesauce (page 22), Pear Puree (page 30), Ripe Peach Puree (page 44), or Plum Puree (page 45). Pork has fibers that are slightly more dense than poultry, so start with tiny pieces at first before moving to a chunkier texture.

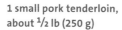

9 TO 11 MONTHS

1 small pork tenderloin, about ½ lb (250 g)

1 teaspoon olive oil

2 tablespoons apple juice

⅛ teaspoon grated nutmeg

MAKES ABOUT 1¼ CUPS (8 OZ/250 G) PORK

- Preheat the oven to 400°F (200°C). Line a small roasting pan with aluminum foil. Trim any fat and silvery membrane from the pork and place in the prepared pan. Drizzle with the olive oil and apple juice and sprinkle with the nutmeg. Bake until the pork is opaque throughout and no longer pink in the center, about 20 minutes. The internal temperature on a meat thermometer should be 160°F (71°C). Transfer to a cutting board and let cool.

- Using a sharp knife, cut the pork across the grain into thin slices, then mince the slices into very small pieces. Depending on your baby's age and chewing ability, you can transfer the pork to a food processor or blender and pulse just until the texture resembles small crumbs; add a little water if needed to moisten.

STORE IT Refrigerate in an airtight container for up to 2 days, or spoon individual portions into ice-cube trays or other baby-food freezer containers and freeze, covered, for up to 1 month.

FOODS TO GROW ON Pork is a good choice for one of baby's first meats. Nowadays, pork is fairly lean, and a good source of iron, protein, and B vitamins. When cooking pork for baby, be very sure to cook it until it is no longer pink.

Pork, red beans & rice

If you have time to cook your own beans, they are great to have on hand for simple combinations like this one; refrigerate the beans for a few days or freeze in small amounts with some of their cooking liquid. If you want to add a little sweetness to this savory dish, try a spoonful of mashed banana.

½ cup (3 oz/90 g) cooked low-sodium small red beans, rinsed and drained

½ cup (3 oz/90 g) Pork for Baby (opposite)

1 cup (6 oz/185 g) cooked Savory Brown Rice (page 76)

½ teaspoon minced fresh flat-leaf (Italian) parsley

¼ teaspoon ground cumin

MAKES ABOUT 3 CUPS (24 OZ/750 G)

- In a bowl, stir together the beans, pork, rice, parsley, and cumin and toss to mix well.

- Depending on your baby's age and chewing ability, serve the beans and rice whole as finger food; mash some or all of them together with a fork to a consistency your baby can handle; or transfer the mixture to a food processor or blender and process to a coarse or smooth puree, adding water as needed.

STORE IT Refrigerate in an airtight container for up to 2 days, or spoon individual portions into ice-cube trays or other baby-food freezer containers and freeze, covered, for up to 1 month.

A LITTLE VARIETY You can substitute Chicken for Baby (page 92) or Turkey for Baby (page 66) for the pork. Be sure to chop the pieces small enough for your baby's chewing ability. You can also omit the meat altogether in this dish; the combination of beans and rice supply a complete protein and makes a healthy meatless meal.

Cucumber, yogurt & mint

When baby is ready for yogurt, try this refreshingly savory dish, which is a nice contrast to sweetened yogurt. Look for organic English (hothouse) cucumbers, which are unwaxed and don't require peeling or seeding. Serve with Indian-Spiced Lentil Stew (page 90) or Root Veggie Stew (page 61) or use as a dip with steamed veggies.

9 TO 11 MONTHS

1/4 medium English (hothouse) cucumber

1/2 cup (4 oz/125 g) plain whole-milk yogurt

1 teaspoon finely chopped fresh mint

Pinch of sweet paprika (optional)

MAKES ABOUT 3/4 CUP (6 FL OZ/180 ML)

Using the large holes of a box grater-shredder, shred the cucumber; you should have about 1/2 cup (2 1/2 oz/75 g). Place the grated cucumber in a bowl and stir in the yogurt and mint. Sprinkle the top with the paprika, if using, and serve. To allow the flavors to meld, refrigerate for 30 minutes or up to 2 hours.

STORE IT Refrigerate in an airtight container for up to 1 day.

FOODS TO GROW ON Babies can eat cow's-milk yogurt before they can drink cow's milk because the culturing process breaks down the lactose, making yogurt easier to digest. Choose a good-quality, organic plain whole-milk yogurt instead of low-fat; growing bodies need lots of dietary fat for brain development.

Fruity yogurt smoothies

Now that baby is old enough to eat wholesome yogurt, naturally sweet fruit smoothies are a healthy and versatile treat, and can be made with baby's favorite fruits. This creamy tropical version is sure to be a favorite with baby.

1 ripe mango

¹/₂ banana

¹/₂ cup (4 oz/125 g) plain whole-milk yogurt

MAKES ABOUT 1 CUP (8 FL OZ/250 ML) SMOOTHIE

- To prepare the mango, stand it on one of its narrow edges. Using a sharp knife, cut down along each side of the stem end, just grazing the pit. Using a vegetable peeler or paring knife, peel each half, then cut the flesh into small chunks.

- Peel the banana and cut into small chunks. In a food processor or blender, combine the mango, banana, and yogurt and process to a smooth puree.

STORE IT Refrigerate in an airtight container for up to 1 day, or pour individual portions into an ice-cube tray or other baby-food freezer container and freeze, covered, for up to 3 months. (Some discoloration may occur during storage.)

A LITTLE VARIETY Try making yogurt smoothies with any seasonal fruit, including ripe sweet blueberries, blackberries, apricots, cherries, nectarines, peaches, or papaya. You'll need about ¹/₂ cup (3 oz/90 g) fruit total.

Roasted gingery plums

Roasting concentrates the flavor and sweetness of summer plums. Plums vary a great deal in terms of tartness, so taste them before offering to baby. If the mixture is on the tart side, try stirring in something sweet such as Applesauce (page 22).

Unsalted butter for greasing

4 red plums, about 1 lb (500 g) total weight, halved and pitted

¼ teaspoon ground ginger

MAKES ABOUT 1 CUP (6 OZ/185 G) PLUMS

- Preheat the oven to 400°F (200°C). Lightly butter a baking dish.

- Place the plums, cut side up, in the prepared dish and sprinkle with the ginger. Roast until the plums are soft and the juices are bubbling, 15–20 minutes. Remove from the oven and let cool for 5 minutes, then remove and discard the skins.

- Depending on your baby's age and chewing ability, chop the plums coarsely or finely. You can also transfer the plums to a food processor or blender and process to a consistency your baby can handle. Stir in any juices that remain in the baking dish.

STORE IT Refrigerate in an airtight container for up to 3 days, or spoon individual portions into an ice-cube tray or other baby-food freezer container and freeze, covered, for up to 3 months.

MAKE MORE TO STORE When plums are at their seasonal peak, make a double batch of these sweet and gingery plums to stir into yogurt or cottage cheese, or to serve alongside Pork for Baby (page 96).

9 TO 11 MONTHS

Whipped ricotta with cherries

Naturally sweet and fluffy ricotta cheese is easy to pair with just about any of baby's favorite fruits. This protein-rich treat is yummy with dark, sweet summer cherries, which are high in beta-carotene and other antioxidants. Fragrant vanilla can encourage the connection between baby's senses of smell and taste.

1 cup (4 oz/125 g) pitted sweet cherries

1/2 cup (4 oz/125 g) ricotta cheese

1/2 teaspoon pure non-alcoholic vanilla extract

MAKES ABOUT 1 1/2 CUPS (12 OZ/375 G) RICOTTA

- Place the cherries in a food processor or blender and process to a smooth or coarse puree. Depending on baby's age and chewing ability, add a little water for a smoother consistency, if necessary.

- In a bowl, whisk together the ricotta, cherry puree, and vanilla vigorously until smooth and fluffy. If you like, set aside a bit of the cherry puree before whisking the mixture together to dollop on top of the ricotta.

STORE IT Refrigerate in an airtight container for up to 2 days.

A LITTLE VARIETY Depending on seasonal availability and your baby's preference, make this wholesome fruit treat using your choice of the fruit purees in this book.

9 TO 11 MONTHS

Big kid meals

In one short year you've watched your baby transition from a helpless infant into an independent toddler. And with that transition comes a giant leap in his eating habits. Right now, your determined toddler is likely feeding himself much or all of the time. He's also ready and able to eat many of the same foods that the rest of the family is eating.

This chapter offers creative suggestions for meals that are both toddler- and family-friendly such as vegetable curry, zucchini fritters, and salmon cakes. Because your toddler isn't a baby anymore, it also provides advice on new concerns, such as when it's time to banish the bottle and how to keep your busy toddler in his seat at mealtime.

Lots of energy

Now that your little one is officially a toddler, he's on the go nonstop. To keep up with all that energy he needs plenty of opportunities to fill his tummy—keeping in mind that his tummy is still quite small—so offer him 3 meals and 2 snacks a day.

The traits of toddlers

While breast milk or formula were his main source of nutrition a only few months ago, your toddler is now eating more solid food and drinking less liquid. He's also likely eating the same foods as the rest of the family.

Erratic eating

Although your toddler is still growing, he's not sprouting as quickly as he did during his first year. Because of this, your once-eager eater may not be nearly as interested in food as he was just a few months ago. In fact, his eating may become surprisingly erratic—you may find that he's ravenous some days yet has very little appetite on others. This is completely normal. In fact, most small children's appetites match their growth needs, which can vary from day to day. As long as you offer him a wide variety of healthy foods, he will eat enough to meet his needs over the course of a few meals (or even a few days). Of course, if you are concerned that your child is unusually picky or isn't gaining enough weight, you may want to speak with your pediatrician.

Feeding himself

Your toddler is also more adept at feeding himself now. In fact, at this point he may not need much assistance from you at all. As he nears 15 months, he may be using his own kid-sized spoon and fork with ease. Dishes like Cheesy Pasta Wheels (page 108), Zucchini Fritters (page 116), Baked Chicken Fingers (page 128), and Mini Salmon Cakes (page 127) will give him plenty of opportunity to practice.

Keeping him seated

If your toddler is walking with confidence, he may also want stroll around the kitchen or dining room while he eats. It's alright to remind him that people usually sit at a table when they eat but that he can get up as soon as he's finished. Encouraging him to stay seated while he eats

Bye bye bottle

If your toddler is still drinking from a bottle exclusively, or most of the time, now is the ideal time to transition him to a cup. Drinking from a cup will keep him from filling up on too much liquid—he needs only about 2 cups (16 fl oz/500 ml) of breast milk or cow's milk a day now—and it helps prevent cavities and tooth decay.

will make meal times more sane for you and also prevent choking accidents.

Getting enough iron

At this stage, your toddler is drinking either breast milk or cow's milk. While each of these is packed with nutrition, it's important to supplement them with the iron that your child needs to fuel his growing body and brain. You can ensure he's getting the iron he needs by:

- Offering iron-fortified cereals.
- Serving meat, fish, and poultry—especially dark meat—often. Ideally, give your toddler a portion at least once a day.
- Making sure he isn't drinking more than 3 cups (24 fl oz/750 ml) of milk a day. Not only does milk lack iron, toddlers who drink too much of it have little appetite for other foods that help them meet their iron needs.

Fat and a sprinkle of salt

Even though your little one may be eating many of the same foods as the rest of the family, be sure to offer him full-fat foods until age two. Fat is important for his developing brain and for other basic healthy functions, and delivers the calories he needs to keep his tiny tummy full.

Up until now, you've been holding off on salt, but your toddler's sodium requirements actually increase after his first birthday, so it's alright to add a sprinkle of salt to his food.

Going to a restaurant

Now that your toddler is older and more mature, you may be wondering about whether or not he is ready to eat in restaurants. Though it may surprise you, the answer is yes. Taking your toddler out to eat is one of the best ways to expose him to new foods.

By watching you sample unfamiliar foods in a new, exciting environment he'll be more likely to do the same.

That said, eating out with a toddler does take some practice. The following tips will make it easier:

THINK FAMILY FRIENDLY Start out in a restaurant that is frequented by families with children. That way you'll be in good company if your toddler gets squirmy.

KEEP IT BRIEF At first, toddlers may find it difficult to sit through an entire meal. Ordering a main course, but forgoing an appetizer and dessert, can shorten table time.

SAY "NO THANKS" TO THE KIDS MENU Instead of ordering bland food from the children's menu, let him sample whatever you're eating. If he really wants a dish of his own, ask your server if the kitchen would prepare a small kid-sized fruit plate.

PACK A BAG OF FUN Pack a few toys, books, and crayons to keep your toddler happy while you are waiting to order or for food to arrive.

Cheesy pasta wheels

This pasta dish is so simple and so yummy, it makes the boxed version obsolete. Small, tender broccoli florets add nutrition to this classic toddler favorite. Cut the florets to the same size as the pasta wheels for equal bite-ability.

12 TO 18 MONTHS

1 cup (3 oz/90 g) dried wheel-shaped pasta or macaroni

1 cup (2 oz/60 g) chopped broccoli florets

3 tablespoons heavy (double) cream

1 tablespoon unsalted butter

½ cup (2 oz/60 g) grated Parmesan cheese

MAKES ABOUT 2 CUPS (12 OZ/375 G) PASTA

• Bring a saucepan three-fourths full of lightly salted water to a boil. Add the pasta and cook for 8 minutes, then add the broccoli to the pasta, stir, and continue to cook until both the pasta and broccoli are tender but not mushy, 2–3 minutes longer. Drain well in a colander, shaking out excess water.

• Leave the pasta and broccoli to drain in the colander and return the saucepan to the stove. Add the cream and butter to the saucepan and simmer over medium heat until the butter is melted and the cream is bubbling. Remove from the heat and stir in the cheese. Return the pasta and broccoli to the pan and stir gently to mix well. Let cool slightly before serving.

STORE IT Refrigerate in an airtight container for up to 2 days.

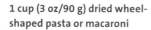

A LITTLE VARIETY You can make this with just about any pasta shape, such as whole-wheat (wholemeal) macaroni, penne, or mini pasta shells. Or, substitute other chopped blanched vegetables, such as asparagus, peas, or cauliflower, depending upon what you have on hand.

Tomato-veggie sauce with pasta

Roasted vegetables give a sweet, well-rounded flavor to this hearty tomato sauce, and hide a garden's worth of healthy nutrients in a dish that is tops with both toddlers and parents alike. Make up to 1 lb (500g) pasta to serve to the whole family, or cook a small amount of pasta for baby and save the rest of the sauce for future meals.

12 TO 18 MONTHS

1 small carrot, peeled and finely chopped

1 small zucchini (courgette), peeled and finely chopped

1/2 small red bell pepper (capsicum), seeded and finely chopped

1 tablespoon olive oil

Salt and pepper

1/2 yellow onion, fincly chopped

1 clove garlic, minced

1 large can (28–32 oz/875 g–1 kg) crushed tomatoes

1/4 cup (2 fl oz/60 ml) Veggie Stock (page 53) or low-sodium chicken or vegetable broth

Cooked dried pasta shapes, such as mini shells or penne, for serving

MAKES ABOUT 3 1/2 CUPS (28 OZ/875 G) SAUCE

- Preheat the oven to 400°F (200°C). In a small roasting pan, combine the carrot, zucchini, and bell pepper. Drizzle with 1/2 tablespoon of the olive oil and stir to coat. Sprinkle lightly with salt and pepper. Roast the vegetables, stirring occasionally, until they are tender, 20–25 minutes.

- While the vegetables are roasting, in a large saucepan over medium heat, warm the remaining 1/2 tablespoon olive oil. Add the onion and garlic and sauté until the onion softens, about 5 minutes. Add the tomatoes and broth, stir to mix well, and simmer gently, uncovered, until the sauce thickens slightly, 15–20 minutes. Add the roasted vegetables to the sauce.

- Let the sauce cool slightly, then transfer to a food processor or blender and, working in batches if necessary, process to a smooth or coarse puree, depending on the consistency your toddler can handle. (Alternatively, use an immersion blender to puree the sauce in the pan.) Taste and adjust the seasoning.

- To serve, toss the pasta with enough sauce to coat the pasta. Reserve the remaining sauce for later use.

  STORE IT Refrigerate the cooled sauce and pasta separately in airtight containers for up to 3 days, or freeze the sauce for up to 3 months.

Veggie quesadilla

For this all-time favorite, chop the spinach and mushrooms finely to ensure that toddlers get a taste of everything in each bite, rather than a big mouthful of spinach or mushroom—which might be off-putting for some young eaters. Serve the quesadillas with plain yogurt and mild salsa for dipping, if you like.

2 teaspoons olive oil

5 white button or brown cremini mushrooms, brushed clean and finely chopped

1/2 cup (1 oz/30 g) tightly packed baby spinach leaves, finely chopped

Two 8-inch (20-cm) whole-wheat (wholemeal) tortillas

1/3 cup (1 1/2 oz/45 g) shredded Monterey jack cheese

MAKES 1 QUESADILLA

- In a frying pan over medium heat, warm 1 1/2 teaspoons of the oil. Add the mushrooms and sauté until they soften, 2–4 minutes. Add the spinach and stir until the leaves are wilted and the pan juices evaporate, 1–2 minutes longer. Transfer the mixture to a plate and wipe the pan clean with a paper towel.

- Add the remaining 1/2 teaspoon oil to the pan and warm over medium heat. Place 1 tortilla in the pan and sprinkle evenly with half of the cheese. Top with the spinach-mushroom mixture, spreading it in an even layer almost to the edges of the tortilla. Sprinkle the remaining cheese over the vegetables and top with the second tortilla. Cook, turning once with a wide spatula, until the cheese is melted and the quesadilla is browned on both sides, 1–2 minutes per side.

- Transfer to a cutting board and let cool slightly before slicing into small wedges.

STORE IT Wrap the cooled quesadilla in plastic wrap or aluminum foil and refrigerate for up to 1 day.

A LITTLE VARIETY For extra protein, spread cooked, mashed beans, such as pinto, kidney, or black, on the first tortilla before sprinkling with cheese. If your toddler is eating meat, add finely chopped, cooked chicken.

12 TO 18 MONTHS

Tropical fruit salad

In the wintertime, when local seasonal fruit is limited, look to tropical fruit for bright flavors and soft textures. This colorful fruit salad is a healthy snack for your toddler when he is ready to branch out into more exotic fruits. The firm but soft cubes make perfect finger foods for dipping into vanilla yogurt.

1 small mango

¼ medium papaya

½ kiwi, peeled and cut into small cubes

½ banana, peeled and cut into small cubes

Whole-milk vanilla yogurt for drizzling (optional)

MAKES ABOUT 1 CUP (6 OZ/185 G) FRUIT SALAD

- To prepare the mango, stand it on one of its narrow edges. Using a sharp knife, cut down along each side of the stem end, just grazing the pit. Using a vegetable peeler or paring knife, peel each half, then cut the flesh into small cubes. Peel and seed the papaya and cut into small cubes.

- In a large bowl, combine the mango, papaya, kiwi, and banana and toss to mix well. Spoon the fruit into a bowl or onto a plate and drizzle with yogurt.

STORE IT Refrigerate the fruit salad for up to 1 day.

FOODS TO GROW ON Ripe mangoes—rich in vitamins, minerals, and antioxidants—vary in size and color depending on the variety. Look for fruit with smooth, wrinkle-free skin and a light fragrance that just barely yields to gentle pressure.

Dining with the grown-ups

At around one year of age, your toddler is likely beginning to feed himself and to drink out of a cup. He's also probably ready or even eager to join the family at mealtimes, if he hasn't done so already. To ease the transition, follow these tips.

The benefits of family meals

Feeding a squirmy toddler along with the rest of the family might seem like a lot of extra work. Yet, including your little one in family meals at a young age will pay off in multiple ways later.

Good table manners

For starters, eating with your toddler teaches him table manners, such as saying please and thank you, taking turns talking, and not speaking with his mouth full. Remember that your toddler is watching everything you do.

Learning from others

By watching other family members, he'll learn to use utensils and to drink out of a cup faster. Sitting down to eat with adults and older children will also make him feel like a member of the family, so he'll be more likely to be on his best behavior.

Interest in new foods

What's more, when toddlers see adults and older children eating different foods, they are more interested in trying them. In fact, children who eat with their parents have healthier diets, eating more fruits, vegetables, and whole grains and fewer snack foods.

Meals for the whole family

While you want your little one to become a well-rounded eater, he may not be ready for the exact same foods as the rest of the family—at least not at first.

These tips can help you adapt his meals, so you only have to cook one meal for the entire family:

- You don't need to sacrifice spice or texture to eat the same foods as your toddler. Simply prepare a recipe as directed, then set a small amount aside for his portion and chop it up. You can add extra spice or any unfamiliar ingredients to a dish after his portion has been removed.

- Prepare a combination of kid- and adult-friendly foods. For example, serve Veggie Quesadillas (page 111) with grilled steak and spicy salsa for the adults or sautéed chard with garlic alongside pasta with Tomato-Veggie Sauce (page 110).

- Add a fresh, leafy green salad as a side dish to nearly any of the recipes in this chapter or the next chapter to graduate a kid-friendly meal to an adult one.

- Double or triple child-sized recipes to make enough food for the entire family.

Tips and tricks for making mealtime easier

START SLOW

If you've been feeding him separately, start slowly by including him in one family meal a day (preferably the meal that's the least rushed). As he becomes increasingly comfortable at the table, have him join you at additional meals.

MAKE FAMILY MEALS SPECIAL

Setting the table, ignoring the telephone, and turning off the TV all let your toddler know that mealtime is family time.

KEEP HIS MEALS SHORT

Since toddlers have difficulty sitting still, you may want to allow him to leave the table once he's finished eating. Store a basket of toys and books near the table for him to play with while you finish the meal.

SET A GOOD EXAMPLE

You may not realize it, but your toddler is watching you. In fact, when it comes to eating habits, attitudes toward food, and table manners, your toddler will follow your lead. By eating a variety of foods, putting your napkin on your lap and saying please and thank you, your toddler will quickly learn to do the same.

REALIZE THAT HE MAY NOT WANT TO EAT EVERYTHING YOU PREPARE

Allowing your sometimes-picky toddler to pick and choose among the foods offered prevents mealtime battles.

STICK TO A ROUTINE

Eating meals at the same time every day will make it easier to keep his meals on a schedule and prevent snack attacks.

GIVE TABLE MANNERS A CHANCE TO DEVELOP

At first, you may find that your toddler prefers to eat with his fingers. Between 15 and 18 months is the ideal time to gently encourage him to use a fork and spoon.

TALK TO YOUR TODDLER

Involving him in friendly conversation will make him feel like he belongs at the table.

SELECT THE RIGHT SEAT

Your toddler is likely outgrowing his high chair. Transitioning him to a booster seat will make him more comfortable and also help him feel like a big kid.

Zucchini fritters

Kids love to dip their food into yummy sauces, and these panfried zucchini cakes, with golden crispy edges and tender insides, make great dippers—your toddler will never know that these nutritious fritters amount to "eating your vegetables." Serve with plain whole-milk yogurt or Herbed Goat Cheese Dip (page 152).

12 TO 18 MONTHS

2 medium zucchini (courgettes), trimmed

¹⁄₄ teaspoon salt

6 tablespoons (2 oz/60 g) cornmeal

2 tablespoons all-purpose (plain) flour

¹⁄₂ teaspoon baking powder

¹⁄₄ teaspoon sweet paprika

1 large egg, lightly beaten

1–2 tablespoons canola oil

MAKES ABOUT 10 FRITTERS

- Using the large holes of a box grater-shredder, shred the zucchini into a bowl; you should have about 2 cups (10 oz/315 g). Toss the zucchini with the salt and let stand for 15 minutes to drain. Wrap the zucchini in a clean kitchen towel and squeeze out as much moisture as possible. Return to the bowl.

- In a small bowl, stir together the cornmeal, flour, baking powder, and paprika. Add the zucchini and egg and stir to mix well.

- In a large frying pan over medium-high heat, warm 1 tablespoon of the oil, tilting the pan to spread it evenly over the bottom. Using a tablespoon, scoop up the batter and dollop into the pan, using the back of the spoon to flatten each portion into a cake. Cook, turning once, until golden brown, 3–4 minutes total.

- As they finish frying, transfer the fritters to a plate lined with paper towels to drain and repeat to cook the remaining fritters. Adjust the heat and add more oil to the pan as necessary. Let cool slightly before serving.

STORE IT Wrap the cooled fritters in aluminum foil and refrigerate for up to 2 days; rewarm in a low oven.

Veggie curry

Serve this sunny yellow curry with steamed rice and plain yogurt. Sweet peas and tender bites of cauliflower provide fiber and vitamins for young eaters. If your toddler is used to spicier foods, feel free to use a curry powder with more tongue-tingling heat. Leftovers make a toddler-friendly filling for mini whole-wheat (wholemeal) pita.

12 TO 18 MONTHS

1 tablespoon olive oil

½ yellow onion, minced

2 medium yellow potatoes, peeled and cut into ½-inch (12-mm) pieces

½ small head cauliflower, cored and cut into ½-inch (12-mm) pieces

1 cup (5 oz/155 g) fresh or frozen peas

1¼ cups (10 fl oz/310 ml) Veggie Stock (page 53), low-sodium vegetable broth, or water

1 teaspoon mild yellow curry powder

½ teaspoon ground cumin

½ teaspoon ground paprika

¼ teaspoon salt

½ cup (4 fl oz/125 ml) coconut milk

MAKES ABOUT 1½ CUPS (12 OZ/375 G) CURRY

● In a frying pan over medium heat, warm the olive oil. Add the onion and sauté until softened, 3–5 minutes. Add the potatoes, cauliflower, peas, stock, curry powder, cumin, paprika, and salt. Raise the heat to medium-high and bring to a boil. Reduce the heat to medium-low, cover, and simmer, stirring occasionally, until the potatoes and cauliflower are very tender, about 15 minutes. If the mixture starts to stick, add 1–2 tablespoons water to the pan as needed.

● Stir in the coconut milk and cook, uncovered, until heated through, about 1 minute longer. Remove from the heat and let cool slightly before serving. Depending on your toddler's age and chewing ability, you can mash the vegetables to a consistency your toddler can handle.

STORE IT Refrigerate in an airtight container for up to 3 days, or freeze for up to 3 months.

FOODS TO GROW ON Sweet green peas and naturally sweet coconut milk are a complementary pair, and a nutritional powerhouse when combined. Peas are rich in iron and niacin and vitamins A and C, while coconut milk—known as a "super food"—is high in fiber, vitamin C, calcium, iron, and many important minerals.

Pita "pizzas"

These little open-faced sandwiches have great grown-up appeal for toddlers, and can be customized to suit your child's tastes. You can even bring art time into the kitchen by letting your toddler "decorate" these wholesome snacks himself. Look for organic English (hothouse) cucumbers, which don't need to be peeled.

1 mini whole-wheat (wholemeal) pita bread

1 tablespoon Creamy Hummus Dip (page 82) or purchased hummus

4 thin cucumber slices

2 teaspoons finely chopped roasted red bell pepper (capsicum)

2 teaspoons sliced olives

2 teaspoons crumbled feta or goat cheese

MAKES 1 MINI PIZZA

In a toaster or dry frying pan over medium heat, lightly toast the pita bread. Place on a cutting board and spread with the hummus, then top with cucumber slices, the roasted pepper, the olives, and the cheese. Slice the "pizza" into small wedges that are a size your toddler can handle, and serve.

A LITTLE VARIETY For a great on-the-go treat, split open the pita and tuck the ingredients inside rather than arranging them on top, making a handheld pocket sandwich. For a yummy Mexican-style "pizza," spread the toasted pita with refried pinto or black beans and top with chopped cherry tomatoes and shredded Cheddar cheese.

12 TO 18 MONTHS

Alphabet soup

This fresh-tasting soup is quick to put together and is a great way to get toddlers to eat vegetables, beans, and pasta in a hearty, balanced one-bowl meal. The Parmesan cheese adds enough flavor to the soup that you needn't add extra salt.

2 teaspoons olive oil

1/2 yellow onion, finely chopped

1 clove garlic, minced

2 1/2 cups (20 fl oz/625 ml) Veggie Stock (page 53) or low-sodium vegetable or chicken broth

1 small carrot, peeled and finely chopped

1 small zucchini (courgette), trimmed and finely chopped

8–10 green beans, trimmed and cut into 1/2-inch (12-mm) lengths

1 cup (7 oz/220 g) cooked low-sodium white beans, rinsed and drained

1 cup (8 oz/250 g) canned crushed tomatoes

1/4 cup (3/4 oz/20 g) dried alphabet pasta or orzo pasta

1/4 teaspoon dried oregano

4 tablespoons (1 oz/30 g) grated Parmesan cheese

MAKES ABOUT 4 CUPS (32 FL OZ/1 L) SOUP

- In a saucepan over medium heat, warm the olive oil. Add the onion and garlic and cook, stirring often, until softened, about 5 minutes. Add the stock and carrot and bring to a simmer. Cover and cook for 5 minutes, then add the zucchini, green and white beans, tomatoes, pasta, and oregano and stir to mix well. Return to a simmer and cook, partially covered and stirring occasionally, until the pasta and vegetables are tender, about 10 minutes.

- Remove from the heat and stir in the cheese. Ladle into bowls, let cool slightly, then serve.

STORE IT Refrigerate in an airtight container for up to 3 days, or freeze for up to 3 months.

A LITTLE VARIETY Feel free to add other vegetables that you have available. A handful of chopped fresh spinach leaves, chopped asparagus, or fresh or frozen corn kernels are all delicious, healthy additions.

Summer veggie stew

This fresh-tasting, colorful summer vegetable stew is a tasty introduction to the earthy flavor and chewy texture of eggplant. Pretty purple eggplant contains generous amounts of fiber, folate, and vitamins B6 and C, among other nutrients. With thin skins and mild flavor, slender Japanese eggplants are a good choice.

12 TO 18 MONTHS

1 tablespoon olive oil

½ yellow onion, finely chopped

1 small garlic clove, minced

1 medium zucchini (courgette), trimmed and finely chopped

1 Japanese eggplant (aubergine), trimmed and finely chopped

½ red bell pepper (capsicum), seeded and finely chopped

1 cup (6 oz/185 g) diced fresh or canned tomatoes

1 cup (8 fl oz/250 ml) Veggie Stock (page 53) or low-sodium vegetable or chicken broth

¼ teaspoon salt

1 tablespoon chopped fresh basil

MAKES ABOUT 3 CUPS
(24 FL OZ/750 ML) STEW

• In a saucepan over medium heat, heat the olive oil. Add the onion and garlic and cook, stirring often, until softened and fragrant, 3–5 minutes. Add the zucchini, eggplant, and bell pepper and sauté until softened, about 2 minutes. Add the tomatoes, broth, and salt and simmer, uncovered, for about 10 minutes to allow the flavors to blend.

• Remove from the heat and stir in the basil. Ladle into bowls, let cool slightly, then serve.

STORE IT Refrigerate in an airtight container for up to 2 days, or freeze for up to 1 month.

ALLERGY ALERT Tomatoes, eggplant, and peppers are members of the nightshade family, to which some people are allergic or have sensitivities. If a rash around the mouth develops after eating tomatoes, peppers, or eggplant, discontinue feeding them to your baby or toddler and let your pediatrician know.

Creamy polenta with chicken

Sweet and nutty polenta is popular with young eaters, and a nice change from the standard rice and pasta. Instant polenta has a creamy texture, similar to cream of wheat, and cooks in only 5 minutes. Serve with steamed broccoli "trees" for a fun and healthy accompaniment that toddlers can dip into the polenta and sauce.

1 boneless, skinless chicken breast half, about 8 oz (250 g)

1 teaspoon olive oil

1 teaspoon fresh lemon juice

1/8 teaspoon sweet paprika

Salt

1/2 cup (3 1/2 oz/105 g) Instant polenta

6 tablespoons (1 1/2 oz/45 g) grated Parmesan cheese

2 teaspoons unsalted butter

1 cup (8 fl oz/250 ml) Tomato-Veggie Sauce (page 110) or your favorite tomato sauce

MAKES ABOUT 4 SERVINGS

● Preheat the oven to 400°F (200°C). Place the chicken in a baking dish and drizzle with the olive oil and lemon juice. Rub with the paprika and a pinch of salt. Bake until opaque throughout and no longer pink in the center, 22–25 minutes. Transfer to a cutting board and let cool. Depending on your toddler's age and chewing ability, cut or shred into pieces of a size your toddler can handle.

● In a saucepan over medium-high heat, bring 2 cups (16 fl oz/500 ml) lightly salted water to a boil. Whisk in the polenta and bring to a simmer. Reduce the heat to maintain a gentle simmer and cook, stirring often, until the polenta is thick and no longer grainy, 3–5 minutes, or according to package instructions. (Watch carefully as you stir, as polenta can bubble up and spatter; reduce the heat if the polenta boils.) Remove from the heat and stir in 4 tablespoons (1 oz/30 g) of the cheese and the butter. Set aside to cool for about 10 minutes.

● In another saucepan, warm the tomato sauce over medium-low heat. Spoon the cooled polenta into shallow bowls and top with the chicken pieces. Spoon the sauce over chicken and polenta, sprinkle with remaining 2 tablespoons cheese, and serve.

STORE IT Refrigerate the cooked chicken and polenta separately in airtight containers for up to 3 days.

Chicken & veggie pockets

These delicious and savory pastry pockets, filled with tender chicken, melted cheese, and sweet corn, are the perfect hand-held toddler lunch or snack. If small cubes are too big for your toddler to chew, shred the chicken into smaller bites.

12 TO 18 MONTHS

1 tablespoon olive oil

1 leek, white and pale green parts only, thinly sliced, about ⅔ cup (2 oz/60 g) total

⅔ cup (4 oz/125 g) fresh or frozen thawed corn

1¼ cups (7½ oz/235 g) finely chopped cooked chicken breast

½ cup (2 oz/60 g) shredded white Cheddar cheese

Salt and pepper

2 sheets frozen puff pastry, thawed

All-purpose (plain) flour for dusting

1 large egg, lightly beaten

MAKES ABOUT 16 POCKETS

- In a frying pan over medium heat, warm the olive oil. Add the leek and sauté until softened, 5–8 minutes. Add the corn and sauté until tender, 2–3 minutes longer. Remove from the heat and let the mixture cool, then stir in the chicken and cheese. Season with salt and pepper to taste.

- Unfold 1 sheet of the thawed puff pastry on a lightly floured work surface. Using a rolling pin, roll out to a thickness of about ⅛ inch (3 mm). Using a 3-inch (7.5-cm) round cookie cutter, cut out 8 rounds and arrange on a baking sheet. Repeat with the second sheet of puff pastry.

- Place 1–2 tablespoons of the chicken mixture on one half of each round. Brush the edges of the round with the beaten egg and fold the dough over the filling to make a crescent-shaped pocket. Press on the edges to help them adhere, then crimp the edges with a fork to seal. Pierce the pockets in several places with the fork. Brush the tops lightly with a little more of the beaten egg. Refrigerate for about 20 minutes.

- Preheat the oven to 400°F (200°C). Transfer the pockets directly from the refrigerator to the oven and bake until puffed and golden, 16–18 minutes. Let cool slightly, then serve.

STORE IT Wrap the cooled chicken pockets in aluminum foil and refrigerate for up to 2 days, or freeze for up to 1 month. Thaw in the refrigerator, and reheat in a low oven.

Mini salmon cakes

Pair these moist salmon patties with steamed chopped asparagus for a spring dinner. The mini cakes make great grown-up appetizers, too—just double the recipe.

1 slice whole-wheat (wholemeal) bread

1 small skinless, boneless salmon fillet, about $^2/_3$ lb (10 oz/315 g), finely chopped

1 green (spring) onion, white and pale green parts, minced

1 teaspoon fresh lemon juice

1 large egg, lightly beaten

Salt

1 tablespoon canola oil, or as needed

MAKES 8 MINI CAKES

- In a food processor, process the bread slice to fine crumbs; you should have about $^1/_2$ cup (1 oz/30 g). In a bowl, combine the bread crumbs, salmon, green onion, lemon juice, egg, and a little salt to taste. Toss gently just until combined.

- Divide the salmon mixture into 8 portions and pat each portion into a small cake. Arrange the salmon cakes on a plate, cover with plastic wrap, and refrigerate for 5–10 minutes.

- In a large frying pan over medium heat, warm 1 tablespoon oil. Add the salmon cakes and cook until golden brown on the first side, about 3 minutes. Turn, adding more oil to the pan if needed to prevent sticking, and cook until the cakes are golden brown on the other side, springy to the touch, and are cooked through in the center, 2–3 minutes longer. Let cool slightly, then serve.

STORE IT Wrap in plastic wrap and refrigerate for up to 1 day.

A LITTLE VARIETY To make a yummy dipping sauce for the salmon cakes, into plain whole-milk yogurt, stir a little bit of Dijon mustard, a splash of fresh lemon juice, and some minced green (spring) onion or chopped fresh dill.

Baked chicken fingers

Don't be surprised if these crispy chicken pieces become a favorite with the adults in the house. Japanese-style panko bread crumbs have a larger flake for extra crunch. Blend plain whole-milk yogurt with a little honey mustard to make a sauce for dipping, or serve with Tomato-Veggie Sauce (page 110).

1 tablespoon melted butter, plus butter for greasing

1 lb (500 g) boneless, skinless chicken breast halves

2 large eggs

1¼ cups (5 oz/155 g) panko bread crumbs or fine dried bread crumbs

¼ teaspoon salt

¼ teaspoon sweet paprika

MAKES ABOUT 20 CHICKEN FINGERS

- Preheat the oven to 425°F (220°C). Line a baking sheet with aluminum foil and lightly butter the foil.

- Working with 1 chicken breast half at a time, place between 2 sheets of plastic wrap. Using the flat side of a meat pounder or a rolling pin, gently pound to an even thickness of about ¾ inch (2 cm). Repeat with the remaining chicken. Cut each chicken piece in half crosswise and then lengthwise into strips about ½ inch (12 mm) wide.

- In a bowl, beat the eggs lightly to blend. In another bowl, stir together the bread crumbs, the 1 tablespoon melted butter, the salt, and the paprika. Dip the chicken pieces in the beaten egg and then in the bread crumbs, turning to coat evenly. Arrange on the prepared baking sheet.

- Bake until the bread crumbs are golden brown and the chicken is opaque throughout and no longer pink in the center, about 12 minutes. Let cool slightly, then serve.

STORE IT Wrap in aluminum foil and refrigerate for up to 2 days or freeze for up to 1 month; rewarm in a low oven.

A LITTLE VARIETY To make crispy fish sticks, substitute strips of skinless, boneless fish fillets, such a salmon or tilapia, for the chicken. Make sure that all the pinbones have been removed from the fish. Bake as directed.

Chicken noodle soup

This toddler-friendly version of a quintessential comfort food is delicious and hearty enough to feed the whole family. Look for tiny stars, alphabet shapes, or *fedelini* (broken lengths of thin vermicelli pasta), or break up spaghetti or linguini into short lengths. For easy storage, freeze the soup in small batches before adding the pasta.

1 bone-in, skinless chicken breast half, about 6 oz (185 g)

4 cups (32 fl oz/1 l) low-sodium chicken broth

1 tablespoon olive oil

1 medium leek, white and pale green parts only, halved lengthwise and thinly sliced

1 medium carrot, peeled and finely chopped

1 stalk celery, finely chopped

1 fresh thyme sprig

½ cup (1½ oz/45 g) small dried pasta shapes or fedelini

MAKES ABOUT 4 CUPS
(32 FL OZ/1 L) SOUP

- In a saucepan, combine the chicken and broth and bring to a boil over medium-high heat. Reduce the heat to low, cover, and simmer until the chicken is cooked through, about 20 minutes. Transfer the chicken to a cutting board to cool. Transfer the broth to a heatproof bowl and set aside.

- In the same saucepan over medium heat, warm the olive oil. Add the leek, carrot, celery and thyme and sauté until the vegetables are tender, about 10 minutes. Remove from the heat and set aside. Depending on your toddler's age and chewing ability, cut or shred the cooled chicken into pieces your toddler can handle. Discard the bones. Add the chicken meat to the pan with the vegetables. Pour in the reserved broth and stir to mix well.

- Fill a saucepan three-fourths full of water and bring to a boil over high heat. Add the pasta and cook until tender but still firm, according to package directions. When the pasta is done, drain and stir into the soup. Remove the thyme sprig, ladle the soup into bowls and serve.

STORE IT Refrigerate in an airtight container for up to 2 days, or freeze for up to 1 month.

A LITTLE VARIETY Depending on your toddler's tastes, substitute 1 cup (5 oz/155 g) cooked rice or barley for the pasta or experiment with different pasta shapes.

Asian noodles

This streamlined, kid-friendly version of pad Thai is likely to become a weeknight staple. Be sure to use a large frying pan so that you have room to toss the noodles with the tofu, vegetables, and sweet, citrusy sauce. Young eaters tend to be big fans of noodles, and the bites of tofu and snap pea are fun and nutritious finger foods.

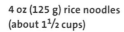

12 TO 18 MONTHS

4 oz (125 g) rice noodles (about 1 1/2 cups)

2 tablespoons fresh lime juice

1 tablespoon ketchup

1 tablespoon low-sodium vegetable or chicken broth

1/2 tablespoon brown sugar

1 tablespoon canola oil

1 shallot, finely chopped

1 clove garlic, minced

1 cup (5 oz/155 g) sugar snap peas, finely chopped

1/2 red or yellow bell pepper (capsicum), seeded and thinly sliced

1/2 cup (4 oz/125 g) plain firm tofu, cut into small cubes

2 tablespoons chopped cilantro (fresh coriander)

MAKES ABOUT 2 1/2 CUPS (15 OZ/470 G) NOODLES

- Bring a saucepan three-fourths full of water to a boil. Add the noodles and cook until tender but still firm, according to package directions. Drain thoroughly and set aside.

- In a small bowl, stir together the lime juice, ketchup, broth, and brown sugar. Set aside.

- In a frying pan over medium heat, warm the oil. Add the shallot and garlic and stir until fragrant, 1–2 minutes. Add the snap peas and bell pepper and cook, stirring often, until the vegetables soften, 3–4 minutes. Add the tofu, cooked noodles, and lime-juice mixture and stir to combine and heat through, 2–3 minutes longer. Depending on your toddler's age and chewing ability, cut the noodles and vegetables into pieces your toddler can handle. Let cool slightly, then sprinkle with cilantro and serve.

STORE IT Refrigerate in an airtight container for up to 2 days.

A LITTLE VARIETY This classic noodle dish is not only kid-friendly, but also really versatile. Add 1/2 cup (3 oz/90 g) cooked bay shrimp or shredded chicken along with or instead of the tofu.

Baby's beef stew

When the weather turns chilly, try this hearty beef and vegetable stew, which the rest of the family can enjoy as well. Young eaters' favorite vegetables are here, along with aromatics and a little pepper for the maturing palate, beef that is fall-apart tender, and plenty of vitamin-rich juices for toddlers using their spoons to scoop up.

2 teaspoons olive oil

1 lb (500 g) beef stew meat, cut into ½-inch (12-mm) chunks

Salt and pepper

½ yellow onion, finely chopped

1 clove garlic, minced

1 teaspoon minced fresh rosemary

2 Yukon gold or red potatoes, about 12 oz (375 g) total weight, cut into ½-inch (12-mm) chunks

2 carrots, peeled and finely chopped

1 medium tomato, cored and finely chopped

1½ cups (12 fl oz/375 ml) Veggie Stock (page 53) or low-sodium chicken or vegetable broth

MAKES ABOUT 4 CUPS
(32 FL OZ/1 L) STEW

- In a small stockpot over medium-high heat, warm the olive oil. Sprinkle the beef lightly with salt and pepper and add to the pan. Cook, turning as needed, until browned, 3–4 minutes. Transfer to a plate. Leave the juices in the pan over medium-high heat.

- Add the onion, garlic, rosemary, and 2 tablespoons water and cook until fragrant, about 5 minutes, stirring to scrape up the brown bits in the pan. Return the beef to the pan, along with any juices accumulated on the plate. Add the potatoes, carrots, tomato, and stock and stir to mix well. Cover and bring to a boil. Reduce the heat to low and simmer until the beef and vegetables are very tender, about 1–1½ hours.

- Depending on your toddler's age and chewing ability, shred or mash the beef and vegetables into a size your toddler can handle. Let cool slightly, then ladle into bowls and serve.

STORE IT Refrigerate in an airtight container for up to 2 days, or freeze for up to 1 month.

FOODS TO GROW ON Full of protein, flavorful, and readily available, precut beef stew meat comes from the tougher parts of the cow and becomes meltingly tender when simmered over low heat, making it easy for toddlers to pull off and chew small bites. Be sure not to let the liquid come to a boil, which could toughen the meat.

Mini meatballs

Meatballs are a favorite with toddlers and grown-ups alike, so it's a good thing this recipe makes enough to feed the whole family. The bite-sized meatballs and small-shaped pasta are perfect for toddlers practicing with spoons and forks. Leftover meatballs freeze well, and can be defrosted a few at a time for a quick and easy meal.

Cooking oil spray for greasing

½ cup (1 oz/30 g) fresh whole-wheat (wholemeal) bread crumbs

3 tablespoons whole milk

1 teaspoon minced fresh oregano or ½ teaspoon dried

½ teaspoon salt

¼ teaspoon pepper

1 large egg, lightly beaten

1 lb (500 g) ground (minced) beef

2 cups (16 fl oz/500 ml) Tomato-Veggie Sauce (page 110) or your favorite tomato sauce

Cooked dried pasta shapes, such as mini shells or penne, for serving

MAKES ABOUT 45 MINI MEATBALLS

- Preheat the oven to 400°F (200°C). Line a rimmed baking sheet with aluminum foil and spray lightly with oil.

- In a bowl, stir together the bread crumbs and milk. Let stand 5 minutes. Add the oregano, salt, pepper, and egg. Using your hands, mix the ingredients just until blended. Add the beef and, still using your hands, work in gently just until combined. Be careful not to overwork. Scoop up rounded teaspoonfuls of the beef mixture, roll into mini meatballs, and arrange evenly on the prepared baking sheet. Bake until browned and cooked through, 10–12 minutes. The internal temperature should register 160°F (71°C) on a meat thermometer.

- Meanwhile, in a saucepan over medium-low heat, warm the tomato sauce. Transfer the meatballs to the sauce and stir to combine. Let cool slightly. To serve, add 1–3 meatballs to each serving of cooked pasta, along with some of the sauce. Depending on your toddler's age and chewing ability, you can break up the meatballs into a size your toddler can handle.

STORE IT Refrigerate in an airtight container for up to 3 days, or freeze for up to 3 months.

A LITTLE VARIETY Add the meatballs to pasta dishes, soups, and polenta, or make mini-meatball sandwiches with tomato sauce and melted cheese.

Mini pancake & berry stacks

These little pancakes are great for breakfast or a mid-morning snack, and provide a delicious opportunity to join baby for a meal that is sure to be popular with the whole household. Wrap any leftover pancakes in aluminum foil and freeze them. Reheat them on busy mornings by popping them into the toaster.

1 cup (4 oz/125 g) fresh raspberries

½ cup (5½ fl oz/170 ml) pure maple syrup

1½ cups (7½ oz/235 g) all-purpose (plain) flour

1 tablespoon sugar

1 tablespoon baking powder

½ teaspoon salt

1 cup (8 fl oz/250 ml) whole milk

2 large eggs

4 teaspoons unsalted butter, melted, plus more for cooking

1 teaspoon pure non-alcoholic vanilla extract

MAKES ABOUT 12 MINI PANCAKES

- In a saucepan over medium heat, combine the raspberries and maple syrup and bring to a simmer, then remove from the heat. Use a fork to smash up some of the berries. Set aside to cool.

- In a bowl, stir together the flour, sugar, baking powder, and salt. In a large bowl, whisk together the milk, eggs, melted butter, and vanilla. Add the flour mixture and stir just until combined.

- Heat a large frying pan over medium heat and add 1 teaspoon butter. When the butter is melted, tilt the pan to spread it evenly over the bottom. Using a tablespoon, pour batter into the pan to form mini pancakes, being careful not to crowd the pan. Cook until the edges are set and the tops are covered with bubbles, about 2 minutes. Using a spatula, flip the pancakes and cook until golden, about 2 minutes longer. Repeat with the remaining batter, adding more butter to the pan as needed. Serve the pancakes drizzled with the raspberry syrup.

STORE IT Wrap leftover pancakes in aluminum foil and freeze for up to 1 month. Refrigerate the raspberry sauce in an airtight container for up to 3 days, or freeze for up to 3 months.

12 TO 18 MONTHS

A LITTLE VARIETY You can use this same batter to make waffles. Cook the batter until golden brown in a hot waffle iron according to the manufacturer's directions. Cut the waffles into strips and dip in the berry syrup.

Making food fun

Toddlers are notoriously picky eaters. So don't be surprised if feeding your once easy-to-please child has turned into a major challenge. The good news: peaceful mealtimes with your headstrong toddler are still possible. The key is avoiding mealtime battles and learning how to tell when your toddler has had enough.

This chapter focuses on ways to make meals with your toddler more enjoyable. Keep your toddler surprised by offering her breakfast for dinner (pages 158–159). Or get her to eat her veggies by tucking them into baked potato boats (page 144) or cheesy calzones (page 167). And because toddlers have short attention spans and tiny tummies, you'll find guidance on portion sizes and how to tell when your toddler is full.

Winning over your toddler

Your little one is eating like a big kid now, enjoying 3 meals plus 2 healthy snacks a day. Yet, don't be surprised if she's picky or even downright difficult at mealtimes. After all, she's asserting her independence in many ways, and that includes at the dinner table. You can help by offering her a choice of fun and interesting foods.

Banishing mealtime battles

Your headstrong toddler may suddenly want to have a say in when, what, and how much she eats. Here are some tips on keeping the peace:

LET HER CHOOSE While you are responsible for deciding what goes on your toddler's plate, offer choices and let her choose which foods she wants to eat. This compromise will give her a sense of control, making her less likely to resort to picky eating.

OFFER BOTH NEW AND TRIED-AND-TRUE Whenever possible, offer your little one foods that you know she likes, but don't short-order cook for her—remember, you're the one running the show. Instead, make sure that there is at least one dish she likes on the table at every meal, in addition to something yummy and new.

SET MEAL AND SNACK TIMES Your toddler may ask for (or even demand) snacks and juice throughout the day or between meals. While some toddlers only seem to want to graze, it's a good idea to try to set standard times for eating meals and snacks. Gently explain to your toddler that it's not time to eat yet, but that she can eat soon. Rest assured she won't go hungry waiting.

Making mealtime fun

Nothing works to win over a toddler better than distraction. Try these tips to keep her interested in what's on her plate.

MIX IT UP Serve breakfast foods like pancakes with fresh fruit or savory egg scrambles with veggies for lunch or dinner, and grilled cheese sandwiches for breakfast.

SNEAK IN NUTRITION Add vegetables to tomato sauce and finely chopped broccoli, zucchini (courgette), or spinach to lasagna, pasta dishes, and pizzas and calzones.

MAKE IT PLAYFUL Toddlers love foods they can dunk. Offer up healthy dips like Creamy

When enough is enough

Even though your child can talk, she may not tell you when she's had enough to eat. Signs she's full include:

- Eating more slowly than usual.
- Playing with her food.
- Getting up to leave the table.

Hummus Dip (page 82), Herbed Goat Cheese (page 152), or Black Bean Dip (page 151). Veggie sticks such as blanched carrots, broccoli, and peppers; whole-wheat (wholemeal) crackers, flour tortillas, and mini pita breads; and chunks of roasted sweet potato or butternut squash are favorites with toddlers for dipping.

DON'T FORGET THE TREATS Ending a meal with a dessert teaches your little one to be a balanced eater, by making dessert special (see page 163 for tips on healthy dessert ideas).

KEEP IT SOCIAL Set up fun lunch or dinner "dates" for your toddler. By seeing her friends enjoy a variety of foods, she will become more open to sampling new dishes.

LET HER HELP Toddlers love participating in mealtime preparation. Let her help while you cook by having her pat dry washed greens, stir a batter, or add pre-cut vegetables to a salad.

Balancing nutrition

Parents often worry that their toddlers don't eat enough at mealtime—a justified concern given that they are notoriously finicky eaters.

You can ensure that your toddler is getting the nutrition she needs by including toddler-friendly foods on the table with each meal. This will provide the nutrition she needs and ease the pressure when you are offering her new foods. At each meal offer your toddler a combination of new foods as well as these time-tested favorites:

Portion perfect

Your toddler may be bigger than ever, but her tummy is smaller than you might think. In fact, large portions can overwhelm your toddler. To make sure she's getting just the right amount of food on her plate, use these toddler-appropriate serving sizes as a guide:

MILK OR YOGURT ½ cup

MEAT, FISH, OR POULTRY 1–2 oz (30–60 g)

BEANS 2–4 tablespoons

BREAD ½ slice

PASTA, COUSCOUS, POLENTA, OR RICE ¼–½ cup (1–2 oz/30–60 g)

CEREAL ¼–½ cup (1–2 oz/30–60 g)

VEGETABLES ¼ cup (1–1½ oz/30–45 g)

FRUIT ½ small piece or ¼ cup (1–1½ oz/30–45 g)

Adapted from *The ADA Pocket Guide to Pediatric Nutrition Assessment* by Beth L. Leonberg

18 MONTHS TO 3 YEARS

- Cool, creamy foods like yogurt or applesauce.
- Starchy foods such as baked potatoes, rice, and pasta with tomato sauce or cheese.
- Soft, protein-rich choices like grilled cheese sandwiches, turkey burgers, or scrambled egg.
- Cut-up pieces of favorite fruits such as apples, bananas, nectarines, and strawberries.
- Mild vegetables like blanched carrots, steamed corn, and mashed potatoes.

Grilled cheese sticks & tomato soup

Grilled cheese and tomato soup is a time-honored favorite. This version takes advantage of kids' love of dipping, with crispy, cheesy sandwich sticks and a bowl of rich soup to dip them into. If you have more than one hungry toddler, simply multiply the number of sandwiches.

18 MONTHS TO 3 YEARS

1 can (28 oz/875 g) plum tomatoes, with their juices

1 tablespoon olive oil

1/2 yellow onion, chopped

1 clove garlic, minced

1 cup (8 fl oz/250 ml) Veggie Stock (page 53), low-sodium vegetable broth, or water

2 teaspoons sugar

1/4 teaspoon salt

3 tablespoons heavy (double) cream

1–3 slices (1 oz/30 g) Cheddar cheese

2 slices whole-wheat (wholemeal) bread

2 teaspoons unsalted butter, at room temperature

MAKES ABOUT 3½ CUPS (28 FL OZ/875 ML) SOUP AND 4 GRILLED CHEESE STICKS

- To make the soup, in a food processor or blender, process the tomatoes and their juices to a smooth puree. Set aside. In a saucepan over medium heat, warm the olive oil. Add the onion and garlic and sauté until softened, about 5 minutes. Add the tomatoes, stock, sugar, and salt and bring to a simmer. Cook, uncovered, stirring occasionally, for 15 minutes to allow the flavors to blend. Remove from the heat and let cool slightly.

- Transfer the soup to the food processor or blender; reserve the saucepan. Working in batches if necessary, process the soup until smooth, then return it to the saucepan. Stir in the cream, cover to keep warm, and set aside.

- To make the grilled cheese sticks, heat a frying pan over medium heat. Place the cheese slices between the bread slices, making sure the cheese covers the bread in an even layer. Butter the outsides of the bread. Put the sandwich in the pan, cover, and cook until the bottom is golden brown and the cheese begins to melt, about 2 minutes. Uncover, turn the sandwich, and cook until the other side is golden brown and the cheese is melted, about 1 minute longer.

- Transfer the sandwich to a cutting board and let cool slightly. Using a serrated knife, trim the crusts from the bread and cut the sandwich lengthwise into 4 equal strips. Ladle some soup into a cup and serve with the grilled cheese sticks.

STORE IT This recipe makes enough soup for 4 servings or several meals. Refrigerate the soup in an airtight container for up to 3 days, or freeze for up to 3 months.

Baked potatoes & lots of toppings

Nothing could be easier and more appealing than a baked potato—tender yet hearty, they are easy to break into bites for little appetites, and the variety of toppings is limited only by your imagination. The recipe on this and the next page will get you started, and give you a host of ideas for other nutritious baked potato meals.

Turkey chili potatoes

2 small russet potatoes, scrubbed

1 tablespoon olive oil

1/2 yellow onion, finely chopped

1 clove garlic, minced

1 lb (500 g) ground (minced) turkey

1 tablespoon chili powder

1/2 teaspoon ground cumin

1/2 teaspoon salt

1 can (15 oz/470 g) crushed tomatoes

1 cup (7 oz/220 g) cooked low-sodium pinto beans, rinsed and drained

2 tablespoons chopped fresh cilantro (fresh coriander)

Shredded Cheddar cheese and sour cream or plain whole-milk yogurt for serving

MAKES ABOUT 3¹/₂ CUPS (28 OZ/875 G) CHILI AND 4 BAKED POTATO HALVES

• Preheat the oven to 400°F (200°C). Using a fork or a sharp knife, poke several holes in each potato and place on a baking sheet. Bake until the potatoes are tender when pierced, about 1 hour. Remove the potatoes from the oven and let cool.

• Meanwhile, in a saucepan over medium-high heat, warm the olive oil. Add the onion and garlic and sauté until softened, about 5 minutes. Add the turkey, chili powder, cumin, and salt and stir. Cook, stirring constantly to break up the turkey, until the meat is opaque throughout and no longer pink, about 5 minutes. Add the tomatoes and beans and bring to a simmer. Reduce the heat to medium-low, cover, and simmer for 15 minutes to allow the flavors to blend. Remove from the heat and stir in the cilantro.

• Cut each potato in half crosswise and cut a thin slice off each bottom so they will sit flat. Arrange the potato halves, cut side up, on plates. Fluff the cut sides of the potato halves with a fork. Spoon a scant 1/2 cup (4 oz/125 g) chili over the potato and top with cheese and sour cream. Let cool completely and serve. Depending on your toddler's age and chewing ability, cut the potatoes into pieces of a size your toddler can handle.

STORE IT This recipe makes enough chili for 4 servings or for several meals; freeze the extra chili in an airtight container for up to 1 month. Refrigerate any extra potato wrapped in aluminum foil for up to 2 days; reheat in a low oven.

Broccoli & cheese potato boats

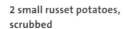
2 small russet potatoes, scrubbed

$^1/_2$ cup (1 oz/30 g) chopped broccoli florets

3 teaspoons unsalted butter

Salt and pepper (optional)

$^1/_4$ cup (1 oz/30 g) shredded Cheddar cheese

MAKES 6 BAKED POTATO BOATS

- Preheat the oven to 400°F (200°C). Using a fork or a sharp knife, poke several holes in each potato and place on a baking sheet. Bake until the potatoes are tender when pierced, about 1 hour.

- Toward the end of the potatoes' baking time, bring a small saucepan three-fourths full of water to a boil. Add the broccoli and cook until tender, about 5 minutes. Drain and set aside.

- Remove the potatoes from the oven and let cool. Leave the oven on. Cut each potato crosswise into 3 thick slices, cutting a thin slice off the bottom so they will sit flat. Arrange the potato slices, cut side up, on the baking sheet. Fluff the cut sides of the potato with a fork and top each piece with $^1/_2$ teaspoon of the butter. Sprinkle lightly with salt and pepper, if desired.

- Top the potato slices with the broccoli and cheese, dividing them evenly. Return to the oven and bake until the cheese is melted, 3–5 minutes. Let cool, then serve. Depending on your toddler's age and chewing ability, you can leave the potato slices whole or cut them up into pieces of a size your toddler can handle.

A LITTLE VARIETY Here are more yummy, toddler-friendly ideas for turning the humble spud into a nutritious snack or meal. Prepare the baked potato as directed above, omitting the broccoli and cheese, then top with:

- Warm, mashed black beans, shredded Cheddar cheese, a spoonful of mild salsa, and plain whole-milk yogurt.

- Finely chopped avocado, minced green (spring) onion, and a squeeze of fresh lime juice.

- Warm lentils and crumbled turkey bacon.

Snacking sense

Nutritious snacks are the ideal answer to your toddler's erratic eating habits. Offering your little one balanced and healthy snacks doesn't just keep him from getting overly hungry in between meals; it's also a low-pressure way to sneak in additional nutrients that he may have missed out on at earlier meals.

Planning the perfect snack

We often think of snacks as quick convenience foods to eat on the run, but sometimes the best snack for your toddler is one that you've had some time to think about in advance.

To provide optimal nutrition and to keep your little one satisfied until his next meal, his snack should resemble a mini meal made from real food. Aim for a mix of protein, fats, and carbohydrates to keep him satisfied and nourished until his next meal.

Most toddlers would be happy to graze and nibble all day long. To make sure snack time doesn't interfere with mealtime, offer your toddler a snack at the same time, two or three times every day.

Snacking on the go

For days when you're out and about, try these tips for convenient, portable snacking:

- Pack snacks that don't require refrigeration, such as mini peanut butter sandwiches on whole-wheat (wholemeal) bread.

- Minimize mess by choosing snacks that don't drip, like mini carrot-bran muffins or slices of banana or zucchini bread.

- Pack in single servings, using individual containers to keep food fresh.

- Opt for cut-up fruits that travel well, such as sliced apples, bananas, or strawberries.

- Store napkins, paper towels, and small paper plates in your car so you won't have to pack them every time you take a snack on the road.

Snack-time serving sizes

When it comes to serving sizes for your toddler, think small:

- ¼–½ cup (2–4 oz/60–125 g) yogurt, cottage cheese, or ricotta cheese
- ¼–½ cup (1½–3 oz/45–90 g) whole-grain (wholemeal) cereal
- ½ slice of whole-grain or whole-wheat (wholemeal) bread
- ½ mini bagel
- ¼ cup (2 oz/60 g) chopped fresh fruit or blanched vegetables
- ½ small piece of ripe fruit

Toddler-friendly snacks

Add these smart snacks to your repertoire to fill in nutritional gaps in your toddler's diet.

FOR CALCIUM

- Half a mini bagel with tomato sauce and cheese, toasted under the broiler (grill)

- Single-serving container of cottage cheese or yogurt topped with pureed or chopped fresh fruit, such as blueberries or peaches

- Small bowl of whole-grain (wholemeal) cereal with chopped raisins or chopped unsalted almonds, and milk

- Small bowl of ricotta cheese sprinkled with cinnamon sugar or mixed with fruit puree

- Applesauce (page 22) mixed with cottage cheese

FOR PROTEIN

- Thin slices of ham or turkey breast tucked into half a mini whole-wheat (wholemeal) pita

- Whole-wheat (wholemeal) crackers spread with peanut, almond, or soy nut butter

- Half of a warm whole-wheat (wholemeal) tortilla, spread with a spoonful of mashed beans, sprinkled with shredded Monterey jack cheese, and rolled up

- Hard-boiled egg, peeled, quartered and sprinkled with mild curry powder or sweet paprika

FOR PRODUCE

- Sliced apples or ripe pears layered with thin slices of Cheddar cheese

- Ripe banana slices dipped in organic strawberry yogurt

- Toasted slices of zucchini (courgette) or banana bread spread with cream cheese

- Roasted red and yellow bell pepper (capsicum) strips with hummus (page 82)

- Veggies, such as cooked carrot sticks and broccoli florets, with black bean, artichoke, herbed goat cheese, smoked salmon, or spinach dips (see pages 151–153)

Almond butter & banana bites

These miniature sandwich bites are sure to be a hit at snack time. Cut them into squares or triangles, or opt for other shapes like circles, stars, or hearts by using a small cookie cutter. Feel free to substitute your child's favorite nut butter—or experiment with new flavors like cashew butter or sunflower-seed butter.

1 slice whole-wheat (wholemeal) bread

1½–2 tablespoons creamy almond butter

¼ banana, thinly sliced

1 teaspoon honey

MAKES 4 SANDWICH BITES

- Toast the bread lightly and spread 1 side with the almond butter. Arrange the banana slices on top of the almond butter so that they cover the center of the bread.

- Using a sharp knife, trim off the crusts, then cut the bread into 4 small squares or triangles. Alternatively, use a small cookie cutter to cut fun bite-sized shapes. Transfer to a plate, drizzle with the honey and serve.

A LITTLE VARIETY Here are some other yummy sandwich combinations that you can try:

- Berry & cream cheese bites: Spread the toasts with a thin layer of soft cream cheese and top with fresh raspberries or blueberries.

- Nutty apple bites: Spread the toasts with peanut butter and top with thinly sliced apple.

- Cashew butter bites: Spread the toasts with cashew butter and top with finely chopped dried cranberries or raisins and toasted coconut.

Veggies with lots of dips

While some toddlers might shy away from sauce on their meal, they love to plunge food into tasty sauces and purees. Vegetables and healthy dips are a great opportunity to turn a fun snack into a wholesome mini meal. Offer trimmed sugar snap peas, red bell pepper strips, cooked baby carrots, and cooked florets of broccoli and cauliflower.

Black bean dip

1 can (14 oz/440 g) cooked low-sodium black beans

Juice of ½ lime

2 tablespoons chopped cilantro (fresh coriander)

½ clove garlic

½ teaspoon ground cumin

½ teaspoon mild chili powder

Salt and pepper (optional)

MAKES 1½ CUPS (12 OZ/375 G) DIP

- Drain the beans in a fine-mesh sieve, reserving the liquid. Rinse the beans and drain completely.

- In a food processor or blender, combine the beans, lime juice, cilantro, garlic, cumin, and chili powder and process to a smooth puree, adding a little of the reserved liquid for a smooth consistency. Season to taste with salt and pepper, if desired.

- Serve with vegetables or sliced bread for dipping (see above and page 153 for ideas).

  STORE IT Refrigerate in an airtight container for up to 3 days.

Creamy artichoke dip

½ cup (4 oz/125 g) canned artichoke hearts

2 green (spring) onions, finely chopped

4 oz (125 g) cream cheese, at room temperature

2 tablespoons chopped fresh flat-leaf (Italian) parsley

2–3 teaspoons fresh lemon juice

MAKES 1 CUP (8 OZ/250 G) DIP

- Rinse and drain the artichoke hearts.

- In a food processor or blender, combine the artichokes, green onions, cream cheese, parsley, and 2 teaspoons lemon juice. Process to a smooth puree. Season with lemon juice to taste.

- Serve with vegetables or sliced bread for dipping (see above and page 153 for ideas).

  STORE IT Refrigerate in an airtight container for up to 3 days.

Herbed goat cheese dip

5 oz (155 g) soft goat cheese

$^{1}/_{3}$ cup ($2^{1}/_{2}$ oz/75 g)
plain whole-milk yogurt

1 tablespoon chopped fresh dill

1 tablespoon chopped fresh
flat-leaf (Italian) parsley

1 teaspoon fresh lemon juice

**MAKES ABOUT 1 CUP
(8 OZ/250 G) DIP**

- In a food processor or blender, combine the goat cheese, yogurt, dill, parsley, and lemon juice and process to a smooth puree.

- Serve with vegetables or sliced bread for dipping (see pages 151 and 153 for ideas).

STORE IT Refrigerate in an airtight container for up to 3 days.

Smoked salmon dip

2 oz (60 g) smoked salmon,
chopped

$^{1}/_{4}$ cup (2 oz/60 g) whipped
cream cheese

2 tablespoons plain
whole-milk yogurt

1 teaspoon chopped fresh
chives (optional)

1 teaspoon fresh lemon juice

**MAKES ABOUT 1 CUP
(8 OZ/250 G) DIP**

- In a food processor or blender, combine the salmon, cream cheese, yogurt, chives (if using), and lemon juice and process to a smooth puree.

- Serve with vegetables or sliced bread for dipping (see pages 151 and 153 for ideas).

STORE IT Refrigerate in an airtight container for up to 2 days.

Spinach dip

½ cup (1 oz/30 g) tightly packed baby spinach leaves

½ cup (4 oz/125 g) whipped cream cheese

2 tablespoons plain whole-milk yogurt

1 teaspoon chopped fresh dill (optional)

1 teaspoon fresh lemon juice

Salt and pepper

MAKES ABOUT 1 CUP (8 OZ/250 G) DIP

- Bring a saucepan half full of lightly salted water to a boil. Add the spinach to the boiling water and cook just until wilted, about 1 minute. Drain in the colander, squeeze the spinach to remove as much water as possible, then chop finely.

- In a food processor or blender, combine the spinach, cream cheese, yogurt, dill (if using), and lemon juice and process to a smooth puree.

- Serve with vegetables or sliced bread for dipping (see below and page 151 for ideas).

STORE IT Refrigerate in an airtight container for up to 3 days.

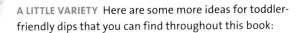

A LITTLE VARIETY Here are some more ideas for toddler-friendly dips that you can find throughout this book:

- Creamy Hummus Dip (page 82)
- Baby's Guacamole (page 50)
- Tomato-Veggie Sauce (page 110)

And some ideas for fun and nutritious dippers:

- Toasted whole-wheat (wholemeal) mini pita or bread, cut into bite-sized pieces
- Blanched or steamed veggies, such as broccoli and cauliflower florets, chopped asparagus spears, trimmed sugar snap peas or green beans, and carrot sticks
- Cooled polenta cut into bite-sized pieces

18 MONTHS TO 3 YEARS

Oodles of noodles

Pasta is a favorite food of many kids, and a favorite of parents, too; it cooks fast, and can be prepared with an infinite variety of sauces, seasonings, vegetables, and meats. Use the recipes on this page and the next as a starting point, and feel free to experiment with other cooked veggies and meats to create your own combinations.

Sausage & tomato pasta

1 cup (3½ oz/105 g) dried whole-wheat (wholemeal) pasta shapes, such as penne, mini shells, macaroni, or orzo

2 teaspoons olive oil

1 smoked chicken sausage, about 3 oz (90 g), finely chopped

1 clove garlic, minced

1 cup (6 oz/185 g) fresh or canned diced tomatoes

2 tablespoons chopped fresh basil

Salt and pepper

MAKES ABOUT 3 CUPS (18 OZ/560 G) PASTA

- Bring a saucepan three-fourths full of lightly salted water to a boil. Add the pasta and cook until tender but still firm, 8–10 minutes. Drain thoroughly and set aside.

- In a frying pan over medium-high heat, warm the olive oil. Add the sausage and cook until browned around the edges, about 3 minutes. Add the garlic and stir until fragrant, 1–2 minutes. Add the tomatoes, bring to a simmer, and cook for about 5 minutes to allow the flavors to blend, stirring occasionally. Stir in the pasta and basil and season with salt and pepper to taste. Depending on your toddler's age and chewing ability, you can cut the sausage and pasta into pieces of a size your toddler can handle.

STORE IT Refrigerate in an airtight container for up to 2 days.

A LITTLE VARIETY Here are some more ideas for healthy and delicious pastas:

- Substitute finely chopped cooked asparagus, peas, and red bell pepper for the sausage and tomatoes, and toss with Parmesan cheese and a sprinkle of lemon juice.

- Substitute chopped cherry tomatoes for the diced tomatoes, and sauté the sausage with chopped spinach.

Chicken chow mein

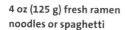

18 MONTHS TO 3 YEARS

4 oz (125 g) fresh ramen noodles or spaghetti

1 medium carrot, peeled and finely chopped

1 cup (2 oz/60 g) broccoli florets, chopped

1 tablespoon sesame oil

2 teaspoons canola oil

1/2 red bell pepper (capsicum), seeded and finely chopped

1 cup (6 oz/185 g) shredded cooked chicken

1 1/2–2 tablespoons low-sodium soy sauce

MAKES ABOUT 4 CUPS (24 OZ/750 G) NOODLES

- Bring a saucepan three-fourths full of lightly salted water to a boil. Add the noodles and cook until tender but still firm, about 8 minutes. During the last 2 minutes of cooking, add the carrot and broccoli to blanch. Drain the noodles and vegetables together in a colander.

- In a large frying pan over medium-high heat, warm the sesame and canola oils. Add the bell pepper and toss and stir until softened, 2–3 minutes. Add the chicken, noodles, carrots, broccoli, and 1 1/2 tablespoons soy sauce and stir to mix well. Cook until all of the vegetables are crisp-tender and heated through, about 2 minutes longer. Season with more soy sauce to taste. Depending on your toddler's age and chewing ability, cut the ingredients into pieces of a size your toddler can handle.

STORE IT Refrigerate in an airtight container for up to 2 days.

A LITTLE VARIETY Using the recipe above as your starting point, swap out the meat and veggies for different combinations your toddler will love:

- Substitute finely chopped sugar snap peas and fresh corn kernels for the broccoli and carrot.

- Substitute thin slices of chopped cooked steak for the chicken, and add 1 minced clove garlic with the pepper.

- Substitute thin slices of chopped cooked pork tenderloin for the chicken, and chopped pineapple for the carrot.

- Substitute small cubes of tofu for the chicken, and teriyaki sauce for the soy sauce.

- Substitute finely chopped asparagus for the broccoli, and cooked, flaked, boneless salmon for the chicken.

Breakfast for dinner

Scrambled eggs make for an easy dinner that is an almost guaranteed hit with your baby or toddler. The soft, creamy curds combine with a wide range of foods from meats to vegetables to cheeses. Use the freshest eggs you can find, choosing organic, and from pasture-raised hens, whenever possible.

18 MONTHS TO 3 YEARS

Cheesy egg with herbs

1 large egg

1 teaspoon whole milk

2 tablespoons shredded Cheddar cheese

1 teaspoon chopped fresh herbs such as chives, tarragon, and/or flat-leaf (Italian) parsley

1 teaspoon unsalted butter

MAKES 1 SERVING

- In a small bowl, combine the egg and milk and beat lightly to blend. Stir in the cheese and herbs.

- In a nonstick frying pan over medium heat, melt the butter. When the butter is melted and foamy, add the egg mixture and cook, stirring constantly, until set but still moist looking, about 2 minutes. Let cool slightly before serving.

Mexican egg scramble

1 large egg

1 teaspoon whole milk

2 tablespoons shredded Cheddar cheese

$1/2$ tablespoon unsalted butter

Half of a 6-inch (15-cm) corn tortilla, cut into bite-sized pieces

1 tablespoon mild red or green salsa (optional)

MAKES 1 SERVING

- In a small bowl, combine the egg and milk and beat lightly to blend. Stir in the cheese.

- In a nonstick frying pan over medium heat, melt the butter. When the butter is melted and foamy, add the tortilla pieces and cook, stirring often, until they begin to brown, about 2 minutes. Add the egg mixture and cook, stirring constantly, until set but still moist looking, 2–3 minutes. Let cool slightly before serving. Top with the salsa, if desired.

Savory sausage & mushroom egg

1 large egg

1 teaspoon whole milk

2 tablespoons shredded Monterey jack cheese

1/4 teaspoon chopped fresh oregano (optional)

1 teaspoon olive oil

2 white button or brown cremini mushrooms, brushed clean and finely chopped

2 tablespoons finely chopped, cooked chicken sausage

MAKES 1 SERVING

● In a small bowl, combine the egg and milk and beat lightly to blend. Stir in the cheese and oregano, if using.

● In a nonstick frying pan over medium heat, warm the olive oil. Add mushrooms and sauté until they soften and begin to release their juices, about 3 minutes. Add the sausage and stir until it begins to brown, 1–2 minutes longer. Add the egg mixture and cook, stirring constantly, until set but still moist looking, about 2 minutes. Let cool slightly before serving.

A LITTLE VARIETY There are countless variations on egg scrambles. Just use your imagination, what you have in your refrigerator, and/or what your toddler likes to eat. Here are some easy and kid-popular combinations of meats, cheeses, and veggies:

● Finely diced roasted potatoes and thinly slivered ham

● Flaked cooked salmon, crumbled fresh goat cheese, and chopped fresh dill

● Shredded zucchini (courgette), chopped fresh basil, and grated Parmesan cheese

● Sautéed chopped spinach, crumbled turkey bacon, and shredded mozzarella cheese

18 MONTHS TO 3 YEARS

Mini turkey burgers

These juicy little burgers are great for birthday parties or play dates, as well as everyday meals. For the mini buns, use whole-grain or challah dinner rolls or biscuits, or use a 2-inch (5-cm) round cookie cutter to cut your own mini buns out of regular hamburger buns, dinner rolls, or sturdy slices of whole-grain bread.

1 lb (500 g) ground (minced) turkey, preferably dark meat

1/2 cup (1 oz/30 g) fresh bread crumbs

1/4 cup (1 1/2 oz/45 g) minced yellow onion

2 tablespoons whole milk

1/2 teaspoon salt

1/8 teaspoon pepper

1 tablespoon olive oil

6 small, thin slices Monterey jack cheese

6 mini hamburger buns (see note above), split

1 ripe avocado, pitted, peeled, and mashed

MAKES 6 MINI BURGERS

- Preheat the broiler (grill). In a bowl, combine the turkey, bread crumbs, onion, milk, salt, and pepper. Using your hands, mix just until the ingredients are combined. Be careful not to overwork. Form the mixture into 6 patties, each about 2 inches (5 cm) in diameter and 1/2 inch (12 mm) thick.

- In a large frying pan over medium-high heat, warm the olive oil. Arrange the patties in the pan without crowding and cook, turning once, until cooked through, 9–12 minutes total. During the last minute or two of cooking, place 1 cheese slice on top of each burger and cover the pan to help melt the cheese. Transfer the burgers to a plate.

- While the burgers are cooking, arrange the buns, cut side up, on a baking sheet. Broil (grill) until lightly toasted.

- To assemble the burgers, place a patty on the toasted side of each bun bottom. Spread the mashed avocado thickly on top of the cheese, replace the tops, toasted side down, and serve.

STORE IT The burgers themselves store well, before assembling. Wrap the cooled burgers in aluminum foil and refrigerate for up to 2 days, or freeze for up to 1 month.

A LITTLE VARIETY These burgers can be dressed up with all sorts of toppings, from sautéed mushrooms to turkey bacon. Mini pita breads are a great alternative to the buns.

Sweet treats

Health experts agree that at any age, a wholesome diet allows room for a sweet treat every now and then, and that holds true for toddlers. While the specter of spoiling children with sweets looms in different corners of our culture and cuisine, there are, in fact, many healthy desserts full of natural, energy-boosting sugars and yummy flavors.

The dos and don'ts of dessert

- Do offer dessert to your toddler from time to time. By serving her occasional sweets, she'll learn to eat them in moderation instead of overindulging because she was never allowed to enjoy them.

- Don't bribe your toddler with the promise of dessert if she "cleans her plate." This suggests that dessert is more desirable than whole ingredients or the rest of the meal.

- Do explore all of the options for healthy desserts to offer baby, such as the toddler-friendly dessert ideas listed on the opposite page. Those with ingredients like fruit, dairy, and whole grains can help you sneak in a little extra nutrition. Setting out a plate of cut-up fruit and cookies or cubes of pound cake together teaches your little one to balance sweets with healthful foods.

- Don't threaten a child that she won't get any dessert if she doesn't eat her vegetables (or any other food she's picking at). This can backfire, sabotaging her enjoyment of healthier foods.

- Do keep portion size in mind. Serving dessert to the entire family in small single portions keeps your toddler (and everyone else) from filling up on too many sweets.

- Don't offer sweets as a snack before meal times. Instead, save them for the end of a meal. That way your little one will eat them only if she's genuinely hungry.

- Do be a good role model. Go ahead and enjoy dessert with your toddler. By eating sweets in moderation, you'll show her how treats can be a delicious part of a healthy diet.

- Don't tell your toddler that desserts are unhealthy. Teaching her that foods are meant to be enjoyed in moderation will help her become a more flexible and less picky eater.

The 411 on sugar

Despite what you may have heard, too much sugar won't make your toddler hyperactive. In fact, over a dozen studies have concluded that sugar (natural or otherwise) does not affect children's activity levels. However, too many sugar-filled foods will fill her tummy with empty calories, and can also cause tooth decay.

Healthy toddler-friendly desserts

These ideas for no-guilt sweets are filled with good-for-you ingredients for growing bodies.

COOL AND CREAMY

- A small scoop of frozen yogurt topped with chopped bananas and strawberries

- Mini gingersnap cookies spread with softened frozen vanilla yogurt sandwiched together for tot-sized ice-cream sandwiches

- Yogurt layered with fresh berries and whole-grain granola for a pretty parfait

- Rice pudding (page 69) drizzled with apricot, peach, berry, or other fruit purees

- Small wedges of ricotta or tofu cheesecake topped with chopped strawberries or pitted, chopped cherries

FRUITY

- Small cubes of melon or strawberries; melted and cooled semisweet chocolate chips make an easy dip

- Organic instant fruit gelatins made with diced fresh fruit, set in fun-shaped molds

- Sliced bananas with whipped cream and mini chocolate chips

- Whole-wheat (wholemeal) crepes filled with chopped nectarines, dusted with a little confectioners' (icing) sugar

- Mini carrot muffins halved and spread with whipped cream cheese

CRUNCHY

- Oatmeal cookies served with a glass of cold milk

- Apple slices dipped in melted and cooled caramel

- Mini marshmallows and chocolate chips sandwiched between 2 graham crackers and microwaved just until melted, heating at 30-second intervals; let cool before serving

- Whole-grain pretzel rods with melted and cooled semisweet chocolate chips for dipping

- Chopped or sliced apple baked until tender with a crunchy topping of whole-grain granola

Pizza party

Pizzas are a great canvas for meats and vegetables. If your toddler always wants plain cheese, try dicing up a variety of colorful toppings finely and let him choose what he wants to sprinkle on his own personal pizza. He'll likely be more adventurous with the toppings when he's the chef, and smaller bits of toppings are extra kid-friendly.

18 MONTHS TO 3 YEARS

Olive oil for greasing

Cornmeal for sprinkling

1 lb (500 g) purchased pizza dough, at room temperature

1 cup (8 fl oz/250 ml) Tomato-Veggie Sauce (page 110) or your favorite tomato sauce

2 cups (8 oz/250 g) shredded mozzarella cheese

MAKES 4 PIZZAS

- Position a rack in the lowest part of the oven and preheat to 400°F (200°C). Lightly oil 2 baking sheets and dust with cornmeal.

- Sprinkle a work surface with flour, divide the dough into 4 equal pieces and pat into circles. Using a lightly floured rolling pin, roll each round out into a circle about 6 inches (15 cm) in diameter. Place two on each prepared baking sheet.

- Spread ¼ cup (2 fl oz/60 ml) sauce on each dough round. Sprinkle with the cheese, dividing it evenly, and top as desired (see below). Brush the edges of the dough with olive oil.

- Bake the pizzas, 1 baking sheet at a time, until the crusts are lightly browned and the cheese is melted and bubbling, about 10 minutes. Let cool slightly, cut into pieces, and serve.

A LITTLE VARIETY Think outside the box when it comes to pizza toppings. Plan on about ¼ cup (2 oz/60 g) total sautéed or steamed vegetables and/or cooked meat toppings for each mini pizza. Using the recipe above, here are some ideas:

- Veggies: roasted butternut squash or potatoes, blanched spinach or broccoli florets, sliced zucchini (courgette), corn kernels, roasted bell pepper (capsicum) strips, sliced olives

- Cooked meats: shredded chicken, crumbled turkey bacon, chopped ham, chopped chicken-apple sausage, ground beef

Cheesy calzones

These little hand-held pizzas are perfect for a lunch box or picnic basket. And like pizza, they can accommodate lots of delicious and wholesome fillings, such as this simple combination, or the ricotta and spinach filling for Lasagna Roll-ups (page 170). Try experimenting with your toddler's favorite ingredients (see page 164 for ideas).

Olive oil for greasing

Cornmeal for dusting

1 lb (500 g) purchased pizza dough, at room temperature

1 cup (8 fl oz/250 ml) Tomato-Veggie Sauce (page 110) or your favorite tomato sauce

½ cup (3 oz/90 g) chopped pepperoni or ham or shredded, cooked chicken

1 cup (4 oz/125 g) shredded mozzarella cheese

MAKES 8 MINI CALZONES

- Position 2 racks evenly in the oven and preheat to 450°F (230°C). Lightly oil 2 baking sheets and dust with cornmeal.

- On a lightly floured surface, divide the dough into 8 equal pieces and pat into circles. Dust your hands with flour and use your fingers to gently stretch and pat each piece into a round about 5 inches (13 cm) in diameter, or roll out with a lightly floured rolling pin. Spread equal amounts of the tomato sauce, pepperoni, and cheese, in that order, on one half of each round, leaving the edges free of filling. Fold each round in half to enclose the filling, and fold and pinch the edges together. Use the tines of a fork to seal the calzones. Transfer the calzones to the prepared baking sheets, and pierce the tops with the fork.

- Bake the calzones until the crusts are golden brown, about 15 minutes, rotating the baking sheets about halfway through. Let cool on the baking sheet before serving.

  STORE IT Wrap the calzones in aluminum foil and refrigerate for up to 2 days, or wrap in foil and place in an airtight container and freeze for up to 1 month. Re-heat gently in a low oven.

Mexican fiesta dinner

Mexican food goes down easy with kids and toddlers, and features lots of healthy ingredients, fun flavor combinations, and yummy spices. Fold any of the fillings here into warm corn tortillas for soft tacos, or small whole-wheat (wholemeal) flour tortillas for kid-sized burritos. Let big kids make their own for more fiesta fun.

Beans & rice

1 cup (7 oz/220 g) brown rice

1½ cups (10½ oz/330 g) cooked low-sodium black beans, rinsed and drained

¼ cup (2 fl oz/60 ml) tomato sauce

2 tablespoons low-sodium chicken or vegetable broth

⅛ teaspoon crushed dried oregano

1 tablespoon chopped cilantro (fresh coriander)

½ teaspoon rice vinegar

Salt and pepper

Soft corn or flour tortillas, warmed, for serving

MAKES 4 CUPS (28 OZ/875 G) RICE AND BEANS

- In a saucepan over medium-high heat, bring 2 cups (16 fl oz/ 500 ml) water to a boil. Add the rice, reduce the heat to low, cover, and simmer gently until rice is tender and the water is absorbed, about 50 minutes. Remove from the heat, and let stand, covered, about 5 minutes.

- Meanwhile, in another saucepan, combine the beans, tomato sauce, broth, and oregano and stir to mix well. Bring to a simmer over medium heat and cook for 1 minute. Stir in the cilantro and rice vinegar and season to taste with salt and pepper.

- Let the rice and beans cool slightly, then serve wrapped in the tortillas. For younger toddlers, cut the tortillas into bite-sized pieces to serve with the beans and rice.

STORE IT Refrigerate the rice and beans separately in airtight containers for up to 3 days, or freeze for up to 3 months.

Citrus-marinated chicken or fish

1 tablespoon olive oil, plus more for greasing

1 tablespoon fresh orange juice

1 teaspoon fresh lime juice

1 clove garlic, minced

1/4 teaspoon chili powder

1/8 teaspoon salt

1 boneless, skinless chicken breast half, about 6 oz (185 g) or 1 boneless, skinless fish fillet, such as wild salmon or halibut, about 6 oz (185 g)

Soft corn or flour tortillas, warmed, for serving

MAKES ABOUT 1 1/4 CUPS (8 OZ/250 G) CHICKEN OR FISH

- In a bowl, whisk together the 1 tablespoon olive oil, orange and lime juices, garlic, chili powder, and salt. Add the chicken or fish and turn to coat with the marinade. Cover and refrigerate for 30 minutes to 2 hours for the chicken, or 15 minutes for the fish.

- Preheat the oven to 350°F (180°C). Lightly oil a small baking dish. Transfer the chicken or fish from the marinade to the prepared dish, and discard the marinade. Bake until the chicken or fish is opaque throughout, about 25 minutes for the chicken, and about 15 minutes for the fish. Let cool.

- Depending on your toddler's age and chewing ability, shred, chop, or dice the chicken or fish into a size your toddler can handle. Be sure to discard any pinbones left in the fish. Serve wrapped in the tortillas. For younger toddlers, cut the tortillas into bite-sized pieces to serve alongside the chicken or fish.

STORE IT Refrigerate in an airtight container for up to 2 days.

> **A LITTLE VARIETY** The combination of cooked or roasted vegetables, cooked meats, and variety of cheeses that you can stuff into a taco or burrito are endless. Try filling burritos with Turkey Chili (page 143) or roasted root vegetables, such as butternut squash, potatoes, parsnips, or carrots. And to make it even more fun, put out an array of toppings for your toddler to choose from:
>
> - Shredded Cheddar or Monterey jack cheese
> - Diced avocado and tomato
> - Plain whole-milk yogurt or sour cream
> - Mild red or green salsa

Lasagna roll-ups

Kids love eating their own curly-edged mini lasagna rolls—a gift-wrapped bundle of protein and vitamin-packed spinach that's pretty on the plate and fun to eat. This easy dish is delicious made with Tomato-Veggie Sauce (page 110).

6 dried whole-wheat (wholemeal) lasagna noodles

2 cups (4 oz/125 g) tightly packed baby spinach leaves

1 cup (8 oz/250 g) whole-milk ricotta cheese

¾ cup (3 oz/90 g) shredded mozzarella cheese

Olive oil for greasing

1 cup (8 fl oz/250 ml) Tomato-Veggie Sauce (page 110) or your favorite tomato sauce, warmed

MAKES 12 ROLL-UPS

- Preheat the broiler (grill). Bring a large pot three-fourths full of lightly salted water to a boil. Add the noodles and cook until al dente, about 8 minutes. Using tongs or a slotted spoon, transfer the noodles to a colander and rinse under cold running water. Lay flat on a clean kitchen towel to drain and cool.

- Add the spinach to the boiling water and cook just until wilted, 1–2 minutes. Drain in the colander, then squeeze the spinach to remove as much water as possible. Chop coarsely. In a large bowl, combine the spinach, ricotta, and ½ cup (2 oz/60 g) of the mozzarella cheese.

- Lightly oil an 8-inch (20-cm) flame-proof baking dish and spoon the sauce over the bottom. Cut the lasagna noodles in half crosswise. Place 1 lasagna noodle half on a clean work surface. Spread a thin layer of the spinach-ricotta mixture evenly over the noodle. Starting at a short end, carefully roll up the noodle to enclose the filling, then place, seam side down, in the prepared baking dish. Repeat with the remaining noodles, placing the roll-ups snugly together.

- Sprinkle the roll-ups with the remaining mozzarella. Place under the broiler and broil (grill) until the cheese on top is melted and the filling and noodles are heated through, about 3 minutes. Let cool, then arrange the roll-ups in bowls, scooping up some of the sauce with each. Depending on your toddler's age and chewing ability, cut the roll-ups into a size your toddler can handle.

STORE IT Refrigerate in an airtight container for up to 3 days.

Index

weldonowen

415 Jackson Street, Suite 200, San Francisco, CA 94111
Telephone: 415 291 0100 Fax: 415 291 8841
www.weldonowen.com

WELDON OWEN INC.

CEO and President Terry Newell
Senior VP, International Sales Stuart Laurence
VP, Sales and New Business Development Amy Kaneko
Director of Finance Mark Perrigo

VP and Publisher Hannah Rahill
Executive Editor Kim Laidlaw

Associate Creative Director Emma Boys
Art Director Kara Church
Designer Meghan Hildebrand

Production Director Chris Hemesath
Production Manager Michelle Duggan
Color Manager Teri Bell

Group Publisher, Bonnier Publishing Group John Owen

Photographer Thayer Allyson Gowdy
Food Stylist Erin Quon
Prop Stylist Natalie Hoelen

THE BABY & TODDLER COOKBOOK

Conceived and produced by Weldon Owen Inc.
Copyright © 2010 Weldon Owen Inc.
www.weldonowen.com

Color separations by Embassy Graphics
Printed and Bound in China by 1010 Printing International, Ltd.

First printed in 2010
15

Library of Congress Cataloging-in-Publication
data is available.

ISBN-13: 978-1-74089-980-2
ISBN-10: 1-74089-980-6

Additional Photography: Tosca Radigonda: page 7;
Ericka McConnell: page 17, 18, 38, and 70; Getty Images:
Jose Luis Pelaez Inc, page 104.

ACKNOWLEDGMENTS

Weldon Owen wishes to thank the following people for their generous support in producing this book:
Carrie Bradley Neves, Elizabeth Dougherty, Alexa Hyman, Ashley Martinez, Lesli Neilson, Elizabeth Parson,
and Brian Stevens. Special thanks to the babies, toddlers, kids, and parents who helped taste the recipes!